A FAITHFUL WITNESS

Essays Honoring David Sebastian's
Heart and Mind for the Church

ANDERSON UNIVERSITY
School *of* Theology

Published by Anderson University School of Theology, June 2014.

ISBN : 978-0-578-14480-1

Anderson University is a four-year liberal arts institution with approximately 2,700 undergrad and graduate students. Established in 1917 by the Church of God, the university offers more than 60 undergraduate majors and graduate programs in business, theology, nursing, and music.

A FAITHFUL WITNESS:
Essays Honoring David Sebastian's Heart and Mind for the Church

Seminary Dean 1995-2014
Anderson University School of Theology

CONTRIBUTORS

CONTRIBUTORS IN ORDER OF ESSAYS

James L. Edwards, Ph.D. (The Ohio State University), President of Anderson University and the School of Theology, 1990-2015

James W. Lewis, Ph.D. (Duke University), Dean, Anderson University School of Theology [Since 2014], Professor of Theology and Ethics

Gregory Robertson, Th.D. (Wycliffe College, University of Toronto), Associate Professor of Christian Theology, Anderson University School of Theology

Gary B. Agee, Ph.D. (University of Dayton), Associate Professor of Church History, Anderson University School of Theology

Guy R. Brewer, Ph.D. (Graduate Theological Foundation with studies at Oxford University, U.K.), D.Min. (Asbury Theological Seminary), Dean of the Chapel, Professor of Pastoral Theology, Anderson University School of Theology

Gilbert Lozano, Ph.D. (University of Denver/Iliff School of Theology), Associate Professor of Biblical Studies, Anderson University School of Theology

Kimberly S. Majeski, D.Min. (Anderson University School of Theology), Associate Professor of Biblical Studies and Christian Ministry, Anderson University School of Theology

Cassie Trentaz, Ph.D. (Chicago Theological Seminary), Assistant Professor of Theology, Ethics, and Church History at Warner Pacific College, Portland, Ore., http://www.warnerpacific.edu/directory/trentaz-cassie/

The Rev. Kevin Early, D.Min. (Anderson University School of Theology), Senior Pastor, Metropolitan Church of God, Detroit, Mich., http://metropolitancog.org/pastor

MaryAnn Hawkins, Ph.D. (Fuller Theological Seminary), Associate Dean, Professor of Intercultural Studies, Anderson University School of Theology

The Rev. Marty Grubbs, D.D. (Anderson University), Senior Pastor, Crossings Community Church, Oklahoma City, Okla., http://crossingsokc.org/

John H. Aukerman, Ed.D. (Ball State University), Professor of Discipleship; Director of Distance Education; Director of Outcomes Assessment and Field Education, Anderson University School of Theology

The Rev. Matt Anderson, MA (Indiana Wesleyan University – Wesley Seminary), Lead Pastor, McDowell Mountain Community Church in Scottsdale, AZ, http://mcdowellmountain.cc/

The Rev. Diana L. Swoope, D.Min. (Ashland Theological Seminary, Ohio), Senior Pastor of the Arlington Church of God in Akron, Ohio, http://www.arlingtonchurch.org/

Arlo F. Newell, D.D. (Gulf-Coast Bible College, Texas), retired editor-in-chief of Warner Press, 1977–1993 (Anderson, IN)

David L. Neidert, MA (Anderson University School of Theology), Director of Student Development, Anderson University School of Theology

For more information about the Anderson University School of Theology contributors, please visit the website at http://www.anderson.edu/sot/faculty.

Significant contributions to the publication of this work:

Dr. James W. Lewis served as the overall project director.

Dr. John Aukerman served as essay editor for all selections in this book.

David Neidert served as the project coordinator.

Kerry Shaw (Anderson University Publications) served as layout and printing coordinator.

Deborah Lilly (Anderson University Publications) served as final copy editor.

Ashley Fletcher (MDiv. '14) and **Amity Rees** (M.Div. '14) designed the cover art.

Financial support: This work would not be available without the support of the Anderson University School of Theology Faculty and Staff, Crossings Church (OK), Fairfax Community Church (VA), McDowell Mountain Community Church (AZ), and Mountain Park Community Church (AZ).

FOREWORD

W hen David Sebastian was asked to allow his name to be considered for dean of the Anderson University School of Theology, he said, "It is the only thing I ever really wanted to do." The wisdom and rightness of his selection has been more than confirmed. And for 19 years he has taken on the tasks of leadership for the seminary of the Church of God with a passion for excellence, a heart for evangelism, and the gift for preaching. He has led change at a time when new delivery approaches were needed to reach a widespread church constituency. He has modeled devotion to scripture and to scholarship. He has cared in a pastoral way for the faculty and students, and has been a loyal member of the president's staff serving the whole university.

As we worked to extend the reach of the School of Theology, expand the Doctor of Ministry degree, create master's level experiences, and move fresh options to online platforms, Dr. Sebastian has had an eye for sustainability, something essential to our times. What was often required was to share responsibilities across a small faculty in ways that would bring the best to students while reducing costs. He was gifted for the work and committed to its importance. His colleagues trusted both his knowledge and his integrity. Dr. Sebastian models the best in leadership.

At the heart of the work of this seminary dean is love for the church of Jesus Christ and devotion to her service. David Sebastian was rescued from a life without focus to become a redeemed and reconciled child of God with purpose. As he answered the call to ministry, it was always centered in devotion to the church as a center for reconciliation. What strikes me is the amazing way David Sebastian was enlivened not only to serve the Lord but also quickened to give his whole mind and energy to the God who redeems. From a youthful life that had little experience with intellectual pursuits, he became one of the best-read members of the leadership team of the university. His writing parallels excellence in his work as a teacher. His preaching excels with clarity of understanding grounded in faithful exposition.

The years to come are promising as Dr. Sebastian turns from day to day administration and teaching to a ministry of inspiration and service within congregational settings of the church. Exceptional successes as a pastor and leader provide perspective and resources for service to the church in settings that are always challenging. David Sebastian is a welcomed counselor and evangelist as he moves across the church. Few in national life know more about the preparation of leaders, challenges that must be met in various church settings, team-building and all it entails to lead large congregations today. David Sebastian is a cherished resource for colleagues in a wide range of settings. These are much needed gifts Dr. Sebastian can give to the church in the years to come as he visits, preaches, writes, and counsels.

In scriptural exegesis there really is no text without a context. So it is with leadership and with the church. Seminary faculty and leaders are keenly aware that they are providing a context for undertaking the scholarship of ministerial education. They are also creating an opportunity in which the art of pastoral service is explored. Occasionally in a teacher, we see a strong model of these understandings lived out in transparency for the student. It is clear to all who have walked the paths of the Anderson University School of Theology that in Dr. Sebastian's life and work, one has an authentic scholar and faithful community member. For that we are enormously grateful.

It is a choice blessing when colleagues who serve with a dean commit to celebrating such remarkable leadership by publishing their thoughts and lifting up the lessons of these nearly four decades of remarkable ministry, first in local churches and for the last two decades, at a seminary dedicated to the preparation of women and men for the ministry of biblical reconciliation. I am grateful that this work is being shared and such an able and faithful servant of school and church is being so honored. To God be our thanks and praise for this remarkable service.

James L. Edwards
President
Anderson University School of Theology

D r. Gregory Robertson has developed, for purposes of this book, an essay laying the conceptual and scriptural path "Toward a Theology of Honoring Others." Those who might consider such a project an act of hubris should give serious attention to Dr. Robertson's essay. The essays contained herein intentionally seek to honor Dean David Sebastian through focusing on dimensions of his ministry that seem to characterize his life over the long term. Dr. Robertson concludes that "God is appropriately honored when as creatures we honor other creatures who have acted to the glory of God." Our efforts in this book operate on the basis of this theological and biblical perspective on "honoring" another.

Through active conversations among the faculty and with others who know Dr. David Sebastian well, we are convinced that *preaching, evangelism,* and *leadership* accurately characterize his life and work in ministry.[1] While these themes are handled separately from one another, they must be deemed interdependent — not viewed as insular and independent of each other. A case might be made that each informs and is informed by the other. For example, preaching is a core practice of the Church — and certainly of the Church of God (Anderson, IN). A goal and purpose of faithful preaching is that people might hear what God has done and is doing in Jesus of Nazareth, through the power of the Holy Spirit. One is called to respond to the Good News of the Gospel, as those who heard Peter's *kerygma* and responded by asking the question, "What must we do?" (Acts 2:37) [Evangelism]. Those who respond to the Good News are born into the body of Christ, the Church, and given gifts. "We have different gifts…If it is to *lead,* do it diligently" (Romans 12:6,8) [Leadership].

President James L. Edwards, in his foreword, indicated the following about the initial call of Dr. David Sebastian to the position as dean of the Anderson University School of Theology: "As he answered the call to ministry [to the seminary], it was always centered in devotion to the church as a center for reconciliation." President Edwards highlights what

---

[1] The reader is reminded that these three dimensions attempt to capture his professional ministry. Those who know David Sebastian well acknowledge the love he demonstrates to his family, mentors, and close friends.

is so central to Anderson University School of Theology — its mission "to form women and men in the ministry of biblical reconciliation." We not only seek to live it out, but it is central in our proclamation (See 2 Corinthians 5:18-21).

In many parts of the African American tradition, we are fond of announcing to the congregation, "There's a Preacher in the house!" As we reflect on the ministry of Dean David Sebastian in these essays, please know that one can shout out that indeed "there is a preacher in the house!" From varying perspectives, we have professors/writers who also are preachers: Gary Agee, Guy Brewer, Gilbert Lozano, and Kimberly Majeski. Take care to hear their unique voices as you read Part I.

Dr. Gary Agee, in his essay "Preach This!" rightly affirms the power of faithfully proclaiming God's Word as the bearer of Truth to the very ways we must relate both to God and to one another. His essay focuses on the seminary's mission statement, and the role that faithful proclamation earns in service to reconciliation. Pray and listen attentively to God's Spirit through Acts 10 — a homiletically generative passage in its capacity to enrich our imagination about the challenges and joys of biblical reconciliation.

Preaching, however, is more than the sermon itself; rather it is the whole process leading to the preaching moment. Faithful preaching requires time — not only time to prepare exegetically and otherwise, but time to listen for and to the voice of God. Yet, how do already busy lives seize time in the midst of busyness to engage in what James Earl Massey calls "the burdensome joy of preaching"?[2] Dr. Guy Brewer offers words of challenge and encouragement to those who labor in such a context. He begins with identifying a most valued quality discovered in David Sebastian: "Somehow in the midst of all the time pressures and complexities he navigates as dean of the seminary, David hears a word from the LORD." As we have come to expect from Dr. Guy Brewer, he provides a foundation and framework that stands against the contrary winds of busyness. In so doing, an intentional (formational) lifestyle characterized by the key elements of "means, motive, and method"

---

[2] James Earl Massey, *The Burdensome Joy of Preaching* (Nashville: Abingdon Press, 1998).

serves as more than just a clever alliteration. It becomes the living fount from which faithful preaching flows. Guy Brewer should know — he practices it.

As Guy Brewer focuses on the foundation and framework of preaching, Dr. Gilbert Lozano builds on this foundation to supply text(ure) and con(text) worthy of a well-crafted sermon. Gilbert Lozano preaches; he loves and values good preaching. Therefore, his essay on "Textual and Contextual Hermeneutics" seeks to serve the church and its practice of preaching by identifying critical dimensions of sound hermeneutical practice. Gilbert Lozano notes this about David Sebastian: "When [he] preaches, one notices that he has spent considerable amounts of time poring over the biblical text . . . [bringing] that text to life for his audience." Lozano highlights important distinctions often lost on careless interpreters of the Bible. Be prepared to learn or to be reminded what constitutes faithful exegesis that undergirds the church's task of faithful proclamation of the Gospel and its implications for life in the world.

One would imagine that all preachers might preach with a common voice. This writer remembers how difficult it was at times to express outwardly what I felt inwardly. I often felt this anguish in graduate school. I held back my comments for fear that others would not find my ideas appealing or provocative enough. Then when someone else stated what I was thinking in a similar way, I remember how defeated I felt in silencing my own voice. Dr. Kimberly Majeski concludes this section on preaching by reminding us that preaching is not just a mechanical act, bringing to the hearers only the results of our exegetical and hermeneutical labors. Rather, God finds proclaimers in many and varied contexts and situations of life. We occupy contexts and many life experiences, wedded together in a sea of emotions, passions, and vision. We live in a world that is multi-cultured, multiracial, and multiethnic; we occupy a world that is gendered, socially stratified, and globally connected. We hear God's voice as the freeing grace to now hear our own — and that others might hear *us*. There needs to be integrity between who is proclaiming and what is proclaimed. How can we preach with passion and purpose without having discovered the gift of "voice"? God's voice of truth and our voice of "amen." A truthful voice because it serves to give evidence that the text one proclaims is not just something we preach but something we first hear preached to us. Majeski challenges and encourages readers to enter the journey to discover or find their true "voice" in preaching. The Church's ongoing life and Christians continuing spiritual formation depend on it.

Preaching demands "hearing," but also commands "doing." Evangelism might be viewed as a way of "doing" the Gospel among others in the world who may not share the fundamental convictions of those who do believe in Jesus Christ as their Savior. In the view of most Christians, there is a connection between faithful preaching of the Gospel and Evangelism. Admittedly, the precise nature of that connection at its worst is a source of disagreement and conflict, and at its best, a multifaceted engagement with others in the broader society. The writers in Part II, "Evangelism," cover a broad conceptual territory; however, what is a constant among them is their love for the Church and for all those for whom the Church exists as both witness and servant. David Sebastian the preacher, in his newly released book on evangelism, illustrates the valued place evangelism enjoys in his life and ministry over these many years.[3]

Dr. Cassie Trentaz, a Master of Theological Studies graduate of the School of Theology and currently a professor at Warner Pacific College, focuses evangelism around the theme of God's comprehensive love — what she calls the "five loves" perspective. Dr. Trentaz embraces the necessity and challenges of communicating the "Good News" in a "postmodern, post colonial, post-Christian context." Dr. Trentaz grits her teeth and spouts her discomfort with the "clumsiness" of the word "evangelism." Employing church history, critical analysis, and truth-speak, she argues compellingly that "love" is more the operative reality all Christians should and must embrace in all aspects of our relationships. Dr. Trentaz's essay feels like a broad introduction covering evangelism's excesses and its hopes.

Dr. Kevin Earley's essay, moreover, seems to add specificity to some of the concerns identified by Dr. Trentaz in her essay. "Urban Evangelism" is Dr. Earley's contribution to the evangelism section. What

---

[3] David L. Sebastian, *Recovering Our Nerve: A Primer for Evangelism in Everyday Life* (Anderson: Warner Press, 2013).

is provocative is that Dr. Earley uses the word "evangelism" without apology. [Can you see Dr. Trentaz's furrowed brow upon hearing and reading the term?] Yet, his essay seeks to help practitioners discover helpful strategies to engage others in the world. While Dr. Trentaz and others may still experience clumsiness of the term, the love and the material realities within urban contexts that Trentaz emphasizes in her essay make for a fruitful conversation between these two essays.

Further, Dr. MaryAnn Hawkins, in "Cross Cultural Issues in Evangelism," comes from a perspective and a heart of a missionary and one trained in cultural anthropology. For those who just want "to save the lost," take heed to this section and more specifically to the skills Dr. Hawkins describes in her essay. Demonstrating love to others in all areas of life and situations is a key theme expressed or implied in the previous essays on evangelism. Hawkins' essay intends to remind all who would "evangelize" or demonstrate the love of God that more consideration should be given to three significant factors: language; relationships, and decision-making processes.

Dr. Marty Grubbs, Pastor of the Crossings Community Church, Oklahoma City, completes this section on evangelism. Grubbs demonstrates humility for his service as leader in this mega-church while equally acknowledging the gifts and passions for mentors (including his father), lay leaders, and others on whose backs he stands and within whose labors he has grown. While Grubbs has faced dire predictions of his congregation's demise, the ministry at Crossings Community Church continues to thrive even today. Why? Grubbs says simply — or not so simply — "Evangelism." He takes the reader through evangelism's various historical moments and how it is now viewed within the culture and lifestyle of the members at Crossings Community Church. In his essay, evangelism possesses a story — a history. More specifically, according to Grubbs, "[t]his is evangelism in the larger church setting. This is evangelism in Oklahoma City. This is evangelism at Crossings Community Church." This is a story worth reading because it speaks of lives worth emulating.

Preaching and evangelism are central to the Church's life and ministry, and to the formation of its members. They constitute major aspects of the ministerial vocation of David Sebastian. The final dimension so characteristic of David Sebastian's professional vocation as a servant of Jesus Christ is "leadership" and leader development.

The four writers selected for this final part on leadership hope to move the reader from the general to a more particular expression of leadership from assessing the season when one's time of leadership in a given setting has come to an end, to viewing leadership — past, present, and future — from the perspective of one who has served long and well.

Dr. John Aukerman has taught, among other courses, in the area of leadership for many years at the School of Theology and is the seminary's longest-tenured statesman. He provides readers with what he believes constitutes effective leadership. For times such as these, his essay "begins and ends with stories of courageous leaders, those capable of bold, life- changing action." Embodied in this essay is good news for people, like this writer, who need to hear wise counsel on effective leadership. That is, effective leadership can be learned rather than viewed as an inbred or hereditary trait. Aukerman argues for the perspective that effective leadership depends on the needs prescribed by specific situations. Read, learn, and do.

Does the age of a leader matter? Does it matter, for example, that a leader is young? I suppose it can. However, Pastor Matthew Anderson, Lead Pastor of McDowell Mountain Community Church in Scottsdale, Ariz., answers that it need not be a grave concern under the right conditions. Using 1 Timothy 4:12-13 as a platform, he mines nuggets of truth to challenge and inspire gifted young leaders to serve the church well and faithfully. He reminds us that young pastors and leaders bring gifts and energy, but they also must heed the challenges that might attend their youthfulness.

The young are among us and with us. As we all know from our years in ministry, the young do not remain young. Dr. Diana Swoope represents one who has benefitted from a long tenure in ministry. As in a relay race, she has both "passed" and "received" the baton of leadership. For this seminal time in our seminary's history, David Sebastian is handing off the leadership baton to this writer. Her essay gives voice to much of what I have been feeling and pondering these several months of transition — passing and receiving the baton of leadership. While she uses this specific transition of leadership in our seminary as the lens, the provocative content applies to the impact of leadership change in many organizational contexts. In her essay, Swoope identifies "four symbolic roles to depict the different ways in which a leader departs and the potential impact it has upon the organization." Further, she identifies factors that mark healthy transitions, and highlights issues and concerns faced by incoming leaders. She is on target in this essay, and concludes that "with great courage, tenacity and skillfulness, this Ambassador Sebastian has shown us all what to do 'when it is time to leave.'"

Speaking of transitions, Dr. Arlo Newell's essay is a brilliant transition between Swoope's essay and the "Epilogue," written by the director of student development, Prof. David Neidert. Having personally known every president of Anderson University and all the deans of the School of Theology, Dr. Newell is uniquely positioned to offer his prophetic insights on servant leadership covering the partnership of the Church of God and the academic enterprise. For both initiates and those well rehearsed in the history of the Church of God and her institutions, Newell organizes his essay in a way that captures the significant historical and spiritual movements in the life of Anderson University and of the seminary. He artfully helps readers to appreciate the nature of the leadership that has guided these institutions over their challenging history. Newell aids us in seeing that the leadership that really matters — especially within the history of the university and the seminary — is grounded in the embrace, interpretation and living out of the church's scriptures and faithful practices. The real gem of this essay just might be in its final pages. You decide.

The transition to Prof. Neidert's essay paves the way for illuminating also how holy calling and spiritual disciplines result in holy leadership; however, Prof. Neidert's focus turns more to the kind of leadership particularly intrinsic to the life of seminaries: they can represent big business. Neidert's experiences are far ranging within Anderson University, the School of Theology, local and state ministries, and local community service. He is conversant in business, leadership, marketing, and so on. However, he possesses a mature Christ-like passion and vision to enclose and re-order the assumptions of these various disciplines above within a mature-yet-maturing Christian character shaped by the life, death, and resurrection of Jesus Christ. Friends, it matters for the kind of leadership that is faithful to life and service in God's Kingdom.

What an adventure lies ahead for the serious reader of these pages! Our dean, our friend, and our pastor, David Sebastian, has inspired these pages by inspiring us in our ongoing tasks and ministries. We know him and we love him as our brother in Christ. Lest we understandably get too immersed and forget to give special thanks to others whose labors we must acknowledge, I hasten to do this. Otherwise, without their efforts, the noble aims of this project go unrealized.

How does one take the diligent work of these writers — with varying levels of skills, experiences, and emphases, and edit their essays with both skill and respect? Dr. John Aukerman embraced this editorial task with grace and attention to detail and timeliness. Thank you, John. Also, special thanks go to Prof. David Neidert for serving as the coordinator for this endeavor. What that really means is that he did a lot of the heavy lifting. He received the approved edited essays, formatted them to fit the specifications established for the broader project, identified and worked with our printer to ensure that all deadlines and specifications were met.

In addition, we have wonderfully gifted students at the School of Theology. We tagged two of them, Ashley Fletcher and Amity Rees, to employ their creative impulses to help us conceive and produce the cover design for this book. Moreover, we owe (besides money) a tremendous measure of gratitude to Mr. Kerry Shaw and Deborah Lilly for layout, final editing and printing. Finally, I cannot help but acknowledge the continuing debt of love we owe to others in the seminary community, whose character and hard work enhances life for all of us. Thanks to our entire seminary faculty, staff, students, and our respective families, for their commitment to Jesus Christ and to our life together in community. To God be the glory!

James W. Lewis
Dean
Professor of Theology and Ethics
Anderson University School of Theology

TOWARD A THEOLOGY OF HONORING OTHERS

Gregory A. Robertson

The impetus for this volume stems from the retirement of the Anderson University School of Theology's present dean, the Rev. Dr. David Sebastian. After the longest period of leadership that the School of Theology has witnessed, the faculty has sought to honor Dr. Sebastian's faithful service to both church and academy through a concentrated reflection upon those areas which have embodied his Christian and academic concerns.[1] These essays, therefore, seek to offer to the church as well as Dr. Sebastian an intentional reflection upon those areas he considered worthy of a lifelong investment. Although I wholeheartedly affirm the foundational value of such research and consideration, this essay seeks to explore a more circumscribed consideration that seeks to orient this endeavor within the larger context of Christian faith and the present and coming of God's Kingdom: what does it mean to bestow honor on someone in a Christian context? Are such endeavors inevitably an ill-advised forsaking of the context of divine grace which makes Christian existence possible, or may we consider a "life well lived" as expressive of God's intention that leads us back to praise the God who has made such a life possible? This concern is clearer and somewhat easier for African Americans or Roman

---

[1] By honor, I mean the intentional acknowledging of the value and worth of faithful service to God and the church. I am indebted (though reflecting upon a different context and practice) to Anne Streaty Wimberly's essay "What Honoring Elders Means: A Call to Reenvision the Church and the Soul Community," in Anne Streaty Wimberly, ed.. *Honoring African American Elders: a Ministry in the Soul Community* (San Francisco: Jossey-Bass Publishers, 1997), 3-17.

Catholics, who have strong traditions of honoring their members.[2] However, a concern should be admitted: should not all honor be given only to God?[3] Can honoring one who has faithfully served the church be acknowledged as a legitimate Christian virtue?

Bestowing honor on others has a strong history in the context of universities, stemming from the rise of the *Festschrift* (German for a "celebratory writing") of the late nineteenth-century. In such works, a scholar is honored through an intentional reflection by one's students and peers upon the key themes and concepts that have informed a particular scholar's research. Such tradition has carried forward into the present era, with *Festschrift* penned for scholars who engage in discrete disciplines such as biblical, historical, cultural or theological scholarship. However, a key aspect of this development is its indebtedness to the original concept of a scholar. In a medieval context, a *scholar* did not denote a specialist, one who knew or could determine how to conduct meaningful research in a particular discipline. Instead, it designated a student who was intent upon learning how to reflect faithfully on any perspective. Therefore, within the context of the academy, honoring one whose life work has made significant contributions to a discipline seem appropriate and valuable. The question that remains, however, is if such honoring can be a legitimate exercise as an act of Christian faith?

Making my proposal even more troublesome, honoring another is a tricky concept, especially for those who reside in North America. For

---

[2] For a North American context, I identify both African American and Roman Catholicism as potential sources for understanding a faithful manner of honoring humans who hope to embody God's Kingdom. In a larger context, I would also include Eastern constructs of *theosis* and saints who are more marginalized in North America.

[3] Numerous biblical passages could be evoked to buttress the claim that only God should be honored. For example, in Numbers, when some of the men of Israel engaged with cultic prostitutes in worship of Baal, Phinehas is deemed worthy of a covenant of "perpetual priesthood" after killing one of those who brought a Midianite prostitute into the Israelite camp. This honor is bestowed on Phinehas because he "was as zealous for my honor among them as I am" Numbers 25:1-15 (NIV).

popular culture, there reigns a "cult of personality" in which everyone seems destined to seek the proverbial "15 minutes of fame." An almost inestimable value is ascribed to whomever can catch the general public's attention. In such a context, is it not reckless to suggest that honoring another person, even one whose life has been characterized by faithful service to God and the church, could in any manner be an appropriate Christian action?

Even with this acknowledged danger, it is my contention that such acts of honoring others for faithful Christian service may be deemed an appropriate Christian act within the context of the church's faith. My thesis, though simple, will require an adequate explication beyond the scope of this essay, thus, what is offered here are initial thoughts (accordingly *Toward* in the title) on honoring another person's faithfulness to God as a legitimate expression of offering glory to God.[4] In other words, God is appropriately honored when as creatures we honor other creatures who have acted to the glory of God. At the center of this consideration is a perspective that God has determined to be honored not over and against the created order but in and through creation.

Unfortunately, as Jason Borges observes, the concept of honor has elicited little reflection within theological discourse.[5] Perhaps the most famous uses of honor in Western theology are in Anselm of Canterbury's *Cur Deus Homo,* translated into English as *Why God Become a Man.*[6] From Anselm's perspective, rooted in the medieval context of his day, human sinfulness constitutes a direct dishonoring of God, whose honor must be restored for salvation to be effectual. So

---

[4] To demonstrate the appropriateness of my thesis will necessitate further explication of the biblical, historical, theological, and sociological aspects of what is intended when a faithful Christian life is honored.

[5] Jason Borges, "'Dignified': An Exegetical Soteriology of Divine Honour," in *Scottish Journal of Theology* 66 (February 2013), 74-87.

[6] For a helpful translation, see St. Anselm, "Why God Became a Man," in *Anselm of Canterbury,* trans. Jasper Hopkins and Herbert Richardson, 4 vols. (Toronto: Edwin Mellen, 1974), 3:39–137.

Anselm's concerns are different from those which this essay seeks to consider, for his concern is centered on the divine-human relationship, instead of the human-human, and thereby honoring God relationship that is under consideration. Even so, as David Brown correctly observes, the concept of honor is not a common concept within Western cultures.[7] So, why would I suggest appropriating such a concept for Christian use? I believe two strong rationales can form a starting point from which to develop of theology of honoring.

1. Biblically, God is Honored by Faithful Human Actions

In Matthew 5:14-16, human actions are deemed capable of eliciting from other humans the praise and glory of God. "You are the light of the world. A city built on a hill cannot be hid. No one after lighting a lamp puts it under the bushel basket, but on the lampstand, and it gives light to all in the house. In the same way, let your light shine before others, so that they may see your good works and give glory to your Father in heaven." In its context, the second person address which began in verse 11 is carried through verses 14-16, so it is the persecuted of verse 11 who are the lights in question. The theme of light was common within ancient Israel, with rabbis, Jerusalem, the temple, and even at times the whole nation serving as a light to "the peoples" (τῶν ἀνθρώπων as found in verse 16; cf. Isaiah 42:6, 49:6, and 60:3). The thought here suggests that as the persecuted stand firm even in the midst of their persecution, God's power at work in them will be a witness to those who have not yet come to faith. This faithful witness can lead those who see it to "give glory to your Father in heaven." What is striking about this concept is the harsh censure placed in chapter 6 on those who practice their piety for public show. Whether in giving, praying, or fasting, if one does these to draw attention to oneself, such actions

---

[7] David Brown, "Anselm on Atonement," in *The Cambridge Companion to Anselm,* ed. Brian Davies and Brian Leftow (Cambridge: Cambridge University Press, 2004), 290.

are condemned and rejected, so why place an emphasis upon actions that will be seen by others? What motivates the actions is the operative issue. Whereas in chapter 6 actions done to bring praise to oneself are repudiated, in chapter 5 the missional intention of the actions make them worthwhile: the persecuted are not seeking to draw attention to themselves, but a byproduct of their faithfulness may be that others who see their actions may glorify God.

Honoring those who have faithfully served God and the church, I suggest, can have a similar effect. The one who is honored is not honored for his or her own sake. Just as in Matthew 5, their faithful service is lifted up as a means of leading those who may not yet know God may come to glorify God.[8]

2. The Christian Life is Ec-centricity

I would suggest that the practice of honoring faithful Christian service is further supported by the unique theological anthropology of the New Testament, especially as it is expressed in the Pauline (and possibly deutero-Pauline) letters: the believer has her or his center in Jesus Christ ("Christ lives in me" and "I am in Christ").[9] Romans 8:1-11 is especially important in this regards (especially the interchange in usage between "Spirit of God" and "Spirit of Christ"). Christians are no longer in, for, or by themselves. Who are Christians? They are those who are in Jesus Christ. Likewise, in Colossians 3:1-4 the believer is instructed to view themselves in the light of Christ's working for and in Christians. "So if you have been raised with Christ, seek the things that are above, where Christ is, seated at the right hand of God. Set

---

[8] This is, in my opinion, a major aspect that distinguishes a Christian form of honoring from the traditional academic honoring that characterizes the *Festschriften* tradition. While they may share many common characteristics, the motivating factor for each is different. Is the honoring done for the glory of God or the glory of the honoree?

[9] See Michael J. Gorman's helpful analysis in *Inhabiting the Cruciform God: Kenosis, Justification, and Theosis in Paul's Narrative Soteriology, passim.*

your mind on things that are above, not on things that are on earth, for you have died, and your life is hidden with Christ in God. When Christ who is your life is revealed, then you also will be revealed with him in glory." I would suggest that for the writer of Colossians these are not mere metaphors, but are constitutive for understanding the new reality enacted in Christ into which the believer is integrated in and through the Holy Spirit. This theme is deepened in Philippians 3:20, where the writer asserts that "our citizenship is in heaven, and it is from there that we are expecting a Savior, the Lord Jesus Christ." Do living Christians reside already in heaven now? No, they are on the earth. How, then, do they have citizenship in heaven? It is a possibility only if they are truly in Jesus the Christ. Similarly, Christians all like the assurance that they are children of God, yet how are they such children? They are so only in Christ Jesus, according to Galatians 3:25-29 (NRSV).

> But now that faith has come, we are no longer subject to a disciplinarian, for in Christ Jesus you are all children of God through faith. As many of you as were baptized into Christ have clothed yourselves with Christ. There is no longer Jew or Greek, there is no longer slave or free, there is no longer male or female; for all of you are one in Christ Jesus. And if you belong to Christ, then you are Abraham's offspring, heirs according to the promise.

I would suggest that this is why Paul asserts in 2 Corinthians 5:16-17 that he from now on "regards no one from a human point of view; even though we once knew Christ from a human point of view. So if anyone is in Christ, there is a new creation: everything old has passed away; see, everything has become new!"

This implies that all good works which a believer in Christ accomplishes should not lead to prideful self-assurance, but to praise of God the Father for incorporating believers into the Son through the power of the Holy Spirit. I would similarly propose that a proper honoring of a Christian's life by other Christians is not only a thanksgiving for the faithful service of the particular believer, but also a thanksgiving to the God whose grace has made said life possible.

Conclusion

Although these two observations in no way fully legitimate the practice of honoring the faithful service of a Christian, they do begin to move us toward an understanding in which honoring the other can be deemed a faithful Christian practice. In Matthew 5, believers are instructed to remain faithful, and in that steadfastness others may come to recognize God's glory. Here, the missional aspect of honoring can be observed: the church lifts up the life of a faithful servant in anticipation of others coming to recognize the God whose grace has made the life possible. In Pauline anthropology, I believe we find another consideration that points to a Christian practice of honoring. Honoring does not automatically lead to pride in the honoree but rather praise to God for the Father's faithful incorporation of the honoree into Jesus the Christ through the actions and power of the Spirit.

PREACHING

PREACH THIS!

Gary B. Agee

In May 2009, retiring dean Dr. David Sebastian facilitated a faculty retreat in which the mission statement of the Anderson University School of Theology was reworked. The fruit of this time of prayer and discernment was, in turn, to guide the seminary in its work in the coming years. As the faculty, staff, and administration met to discuss how the school might best serve the church, a growing sense of excitement emerged around the results of this collaborative effort. *The mission of the Anderson University School of Theology is to form women and men for the ministry of biblical reconciliation.*

The above articulated statement reemphasizes a common theme important in the history of the Church of God Reformation Movement, which is the need for all people to be reconciled or to be brought into right standing with God. A survey of our history demonstrates that for early Church of God leaders, including D.S. Warner and Barney Warren, the work of urging people to be saved was of primary importance. This soteriological aim is also very much represented in the earliest published hymnody of the Gospel Trumpet Company. Getting right with God, however, does not exhaust the meaning of biblical reconciliation.

In early 2013, Dr. Greg Robertson, associate professor of Christian theology at the School of Theology, was charged with writing a reflection of the seminary's mission statement. In this same document, he rightly pointed out the fact that misconceptions regarding the work of reconciliation must be avoided. Robertson specifically addressed the tendency in North American evangelicalism to reduce the work of reconciliation to include only the reparation of one's relationship to God.

It becomes clear, therefore, that in the drafting of the above statement the aim of the faculty was to foreground another key aspect of the work of Christian mission, a work not always emphasized in the Movement. In short, the statement was more broadly worded so as to address fractured relationships which too often divide God's children. Such a missional focus necessarily acknowledges all of the ways humans wrongly comport themselves to others. In training a generation of Christian leaders to commit to biblical reconciliation, it might be expected that injustice in all of its sordid and community bursting forms would need to be considered, for example, all forms of exploitation as well as biases and prejudices based on class, race, gender, ethnicity, body type, sexual orientation, tribal affiliation, caste, geographic identity, etc.

Robertson correctly posits that the work of biblical reconciliation offers much promise and hope. What is equally apparent is the fact that such a noble aim will also require us to be stretched and reoriented to an alternative value system, one which inspires and promises new ways of interrelating under God. Those who desire such an opportunity for reorientation need only to look to the proclamation of the word of God, a word which always exposes and brings to light the broken ways we interrelate. This is certainly true for those who fellowship in the Church of God (Anderson) or in other biblically based traditions which celebrate the normative character of God's word. Care must be taken, however, to allow the word to go forth without domesticating it through our tired and sometimes neatly packaged hermeneutical formulas. In other words, we must proclaim it and let the living word bring to light the ways we relate not only to the Divine but also to one another.

For the sake of biblical reconciliation then, who among us will stand and preach a word which takes seriously the sin of ethnocentrism, self-righteousness, or exploitation? Who will proclaim for us a gospel that leads to a time of Spirit-stretching transformation, always a prerequisite to reconciliation? For those pulpiteers among us who might courageously take up this challenge, might I propose a text pregnant with homiletic possibility? I suggest the story of Cornelius and Peter from the Acts of the Apostles. Preach this!

Acts of the Apostles: *A Theme*

The account of Peter's meeting with Cornelius (Acts 10) details the story of an initially reluctant apostle who, though in some measure unfit for the task, eventually surrendered to God's leading and gave witness to the life and work of Jesus. Spreading the message of Jesus through witness constitutes the primary theme of this same book. Yet throughout the text, it is clear that the witness given by those who are followers of Jesus was not one conditioned by mere human ingenuity. Rather, it was a witness empowered by the Holy Spirit, as is evident in this story.

Cornelius

In this account, God, who cannot be expected to be held hostage to our cultural hang-ups, was attending the prayers of Cornelius, a Roman centurion. But in the minds of Peter and the Jewish Christians who had been enculturated in first century Palestine, the possibility that God would be present and attentive to such a one as Cornelius seemed beyond conception, even though this same individual was a man who cultivated his relationship with God in prayer, and neglected not his obligations to those individuals in need of a helping hand.

One who preaches this text then, helps us remember the unsettling truth that God is judge and not us; that it is a matter of divine prerogative who is received and who is chosen. Moreover, our well-constructed formulas and cocksure schemes of gaining favor with the Divine are brought into question by the account. If this passage does nothing else, it should remind the hearer of God's word that the followers of Christ comfortably corralled in the Christian fold hold no monopoly on the love and mercy of God.

Perhaps equally unsettling should be the obvious fact that Cornelius, a non-Jew, moved with less resistance to God when instructed as to what was required of him. For when he was directed to call for Peter in order that he and his household might be more thoroughly instructed on matters of faith, Cornelius did so immediately and without rebuttal. In this story, the same cannot be said of the apostle of Jesus.

Peter: *A Reluctant Witness*

In the text, the famished Peter is the next to be introduced. While he waited for a meal to be prepared on his behalf, he went to prayer. In this respect, his piety merely matches that of Cornelius. While in prayer, Peter was carried away into a trance-like state. It was while the apostle was in this condition that he saw a vision of a sheet coming down from heaven. In it was a variety of unclean birds, beasts and reptiles forbidden by Jewish law. What was so disconcerting for Peter, according to the account, was the directive he then received, instruction clearly of divine origin. He was told to "rise, kill, and eat."

Peter became confused. On the one hand, he felt God directing him to eat of this unclean smorgasbord of beasts. On the other hand, he had been trained and taught the Law of Moses, which seemed quite clear on the matter. After all, one could read plainly the proscriptions against eating unclean animals from Leviticus 11 or Deuteronomy 14:3-20.

As Peter would learn later in the narrative, this encounter was about much more than his diet. Rather, it was to bring to the surface a sinful posture, a way of thinking and feeling about Gentiles that impeded the work of the Lord. The vision, then, served to help this preacher of the good news of Jesus Christ to become the agent of reconciliation that God intended. It should be noted that Cornelius apparently needed no such cleansing encounter.

As uncomfortable as it was, it is important to point out that it was during this time of cognitive dissonance that Peter went through a time of real "Spirit-stretching" transformation. Instead of making Peter an effective or powerful speaker, however, God was stretching the imagination and heart of the apostle. In this time of growth, Peter would have to let go of his feeling of religious and cultural superiority. Moreover, all the conditioning, all the degrading opinions he held toward the Gentiles, all the prejudices and stereotypes which had been part and parcel to his upbringing had to be addressed. Such a conversion of the heart was needful for the apostle. For Peter needed to learn to love the world God already loved. Only with the possession of this type of reconciling love would Peter be fit to help establish a Christian community of the character described in Galatians 3:26-28, a fellowship where no discriminating distinction can be made between Jew and Gentile, male or female, slave or free person.

In the encounter between Peter and Cornelius, it is possible to imagine and speculate as to why Peter showed such reluctance to carry out the heavenly directive he received while on the rooftop. What Peter was up against, however, was the sum total of a lifetime of conditioning which supported the notion that non-Jews were somehow less than. Perhaps it is a bit easier to give compassion to the apostle when we realize that all individuals go through such a process of socialization. Some of this training is good. On the other hand, some of the formal and informal instruction we receive necessitates house cleaning time and again as we attempt to possess the mind of Christ.

For one who preaches this text it may be helpful to note the fact that Cornelius was told to ask that Peter come to him. If we then imagine Peter as a representative of the church, then it appears that the primary onus for rapprochement, for addressing the distance between all varieties of us and them, rests with God's people. We are agents of biblical reconciliation.

Though Peter seemed to be unresolved as to how to reconcile the Spirit's work with his own understanding of what it meant to be a pious follower of Jesus, nonetheless he obeyed the God who spoke to him. This is the only proper response for the disciple of Jesus. When Peter then arrived at the house of Cornelius, his host fell at the apostle's feet. From Cornelius' perspective it seems a predictable response considering that Peter's name was known in heaven. But Peter had learned his lesson. He was quick to put himself on the same plane as Cornelius, "I am a man too."

During Peter's exchange with his host, Cornelius, the apostle brought to the surface a troubling internal dilemma which he faced in coming to see this Gentile. He said that though his understanding of the Law had forbidden such an intimate encounter with a non-Jew, God had showed him his error. Here Peter revealed a hermeneutical heritage which, as mind boggling as it sounds, actually hindered the work of the Lord. Those who dare to preach this potentially transformative text will do well to give some thought to Peter's misguided commitment to the Jewish Law. Let us not forget that Christian history is littered with examples of hermeneutical sophistries employed to, in effect, hold up or even negate the work of the Lord. One such example is the manner in which the Bible was used in support of the institution of human bondage.

In v. 28, Peter stated that it was against the Jewish Law to associate with a Gentile; at the same time, the Lord had shown him that he could not call anyone impure or unclean. This revelation from the Lord, this new understanding of how the follower of Jesus was to comport himself to the Gentile, had been the cause of a great deal of cognitive dissonance. In time, Peter was willing to be stretched by the Spirit. Peter articulated the insight gained from the Spirit-stretching exercise from which he has just emerged. "I now realize how true it is that God does not show favoritism" (Acts 10:34-35). With such a realization, Peter was now ready to be a witness for the Lord not only to the Jew, but also now to the non-Jew.

After sharing the message of Jesus, our Lord's baptism, his work in the world, his efficacious death on the cross, and his triumphant resurrection with those assembled under the roof of Cornelius, something beautiful occurred. The Holy Spirit fell on those Jews and Gentiles together in that reconciled assembly. God had indeed showed no favoritism.

A Challenge

For those who leave this seminary to go out into our polarized and fractured world with a heart for biblical reconciliation, preach this message! Perhaps we too can be Spirit-stretched, we too can be reconciled to God. We too can be a part of a community of followers of Jesus unmolested by the divisions which set one against another.

PREACHING IN THE MIDST OF BUSYNESS

Guy R. Brewer

It is an honor to contribute to this book in celebration of the life and ministry of David Sebastian, my friend, colleague, and dean. In serving under Dr. Sebastian's leadership for the past several years, I have been continually impressed by his steady and wise ways. No matter the details of a situation, he can be counted on for a word of guidance and assurance that is more than one expected. I have had the sense that David surprises himself at times, speaking insights that he did not know he had. He speaks as one who is listening for a word from beyond himself, a Word from the Lord. This has been especially true in his preaching ministry.

When I come to hear David Sebastian preach, my expectation is to hear a sermon that is faithful to a biblical text and expertly crafted. He never disappoints. To the uninitiated, David's preaching acumen might be attributed to his gifts, diligence, and love of proclamation. All of these factors are involved. And yet, I sense an "X" factor in David Sebastian that may be his finest quality. Somehow in the midst of all the time pressures and complexities he navigates as dean of the seminary, David hears a Word from the Lord. He has not allowed the "white noise" of life to deafen him. What an example of faithful preaching in the midst of busyness Dr. Sebastian has given us.

To hear a Word from God requires a lifestyle of intentional listening. I am reminded of the legendary practices in fourth century desert communities that were intended to combat distraction in the preaching life. According to lore, the standard practice in some monastic communities was to insist that the Sunday preacher spend the week prior to preaching in total isolation. On Monday at dawn, community members would tie a rope around the preacher's waist and lower him into a dry well. Throughout the week, three times a day, they would lower food and water to the preacher, but he remained in the deep hollow of the well, meditating on the Word of God. At dawn on Sunday, they would pull the preacher out of the well, with the comment, "Go, preach the Word!"

What an image of the preaching lifestyle: Stuck in a well for six straight days, just you and the Word of God. Imagine yourself at the bottom of that well forty feet below ground. At that depth, it is always chilly, even in the middle of a desert. Although the sun shines brightly above ground, it is total darkness at the bottom of the well. You cannot see your hand in front of your face. You light a candle that community members have mercifully included with your provisions. For the next week there is nothing to do but meditate on the Scriptures by the light of that flickering flame. To the extent that this legend is true, I wonder how the preacher kept his sanity for a week of solitary confinement, let alone for life down the well week after week, year after year.

Dennis Kinlaw echoed the worldview behind these ascetical practices when he wrote, "The greatest problem in preaching is not the preparation of the sermon but the preparation of the preacher."[1] Here is the rub. A leader like David Sebastian cannot spend all week sequestered from others. For 19 years he has been called upon to preach in the midst of an overwhelming schedule. How has he managed to preach so effectively under such adverse conditions? Dr. Sebastian has prepared the preacher as the first step in preparing the sermon. His example is a living answer to three questions:

1. What are the *means* of preaching?
2. What is the *motive* of preaching?
3. What is the *method* of preaching?

---

[1] Dennis F. Kinlaw, *Preaching in the Spirit: A Preacher Looks for Something That Human Energy Cannot Provide* (Wilmore, KY: Francis Asbury Society, 1985), 17.

Those who hear David Sebastian's preaching universally remark, "He spoke from the heart." Of course, he did. Great preaching is an overflow of the heart: "Out of the overflow of his heart his mouth speaks" (Luke 6:45). The preacher's first concern in the ministry of proclamation is the condition of his or her own heart. To place the life of the heart as front and center is a particular challenge in academic communities in which the life of the mind is given primacy. And yet, preaching is a relational connection before it becomes an educational or rhetorical experience.[2]

As such, relational connection – speaking heart to heart – is the communicative means of preaching. Before it is public speech or the communication of information, preaching is a conversation among friends.[3] The preacher expresses his or her priority on connectivity through genuine love for people and for God. Preparation to preach involves a "sacred triangle" in which one brings together three loves: a love for people, a love for Christ, and a love for the task of preaching.[4]

Before the first word is uttered, the preacher must be committed to listening carefully to God, to his or her own heart, and to the community of faith. In this sense, one acts as an articulator of inner events who gives language to the deep yearnings of the heart.[5] Such a role requires active listening, contemplation, and discernment.

If the means of preaching is the life of the heart, the motive of preaching is transformation of listeners. The point of sermons is change, qualitative life change in which people are moving toward conformation into the image of Christ. Such genuine transformation involves a change of heart, a seismic shift in the inner core of persons. In a fundamental sense, preaching is a word of *agape* love with the potential to change lives.

---

[2] Burton Z. Cooper and John S. McClure, *Claiming Theology in the Pulpit* (Louisville: Westminster John Knox, 2003), 10-11.

[3] Lucy Atkinson Rose, *Sharing the Word: Preaching in the Roundtable Church* (Louisville: Westminster John Knox, 1997), 121.

[4] Ellsworth J. Kalas, *Preaching from the Soul* (Nashville: Abingdon, 2003), 27-34.

[5] Henri Nouwen, *Creative Ministry* (New York: Image Books, 1991), 21-40.

The effective preacher speaks as a friend of Jesus and child of God. That is to say, the motivation to call others into a genuine relationship with God arises from the preacher's intimacy with God. In a sense, the sermon invites listeners into God's circle of close friends. Regardless of the content of the sermon, the tone includes elements of genuine intimacy with Christ.

Since preaching seeks transformation of the core self, the primary locus of sermons is the life of the heart. To be effective, one cannot be content to preach in ways that appeal only to the intellect. Likewise, the preacher is not simply seeking an emotional response from the congregation. The point of preaching is to connect the heart of the congregation with the heart of God. As Henri Nouwen suggests, the beginning point of Christian discipleship is when a person hears the message from God, "You are my beloved."[6]

Of equal importance, one who preaches well has confidence in the efficacy of the Word of God to transform lives. God rarely speaks in an audible voice. Instead, God has chosen to use preachers as partners in translating the *logos,* the eternal Word of God for all humanity, into a *rhema,* a personal word from God to particular people at specific times and places. As David Yonggi Cho suggests, the experience of the *rhema* is the "fourth dimension" of life in which the experience of the Holy Spirit works a new creation.[7]

Does David Sebastian model a particular method to the madness of preaching? Beyond techniques or certain practices, his methodology for preaching might be characterized as incarnational presence. Such pulpit presence is an embodiment of "The Word made flesh." Incarnational presence points to a confluence of genuineness, intimacy, immediacy, and inspiration that irresistibly connects with the deep needs of others.

Dr. Paul Brand, long-term president and teacher at the Christian Medical College in Vellore, India, recounts a visit from his friend,

---

[6] Henri Nouwen, *Life of the Beloved: Spiritual Living in a Secular World* (New York: Crossroads, 2001).

[7] David Yonggi Cho, *The Fourth Dimension, Volume II* (Gainesville, FL: Bridge-Logos, 2002), 35-37.

Abbé Pierre. Father Pierre was a French monk renowned for founding Emmaus, a ministry to homeless people and refugees around the world. Following the custom of the medical college, Dr. Brand invited Abbé Pierre to offer a few minutes of comments during the students' community lunch. Since none of the students spoke French, Abbé Pierre spoke to the students with the aid of a translator. As he became more passionate in his comments about the responsibility of the medical community to the poor, Abbé began to speak faster and faster, making it impossible for the translator to keep up. He continued speaking without translation for the next fifteen minutes. The medical students stopped eating and listened with rapt attention. When Abbé Pierre finished speaking, the students gave him a standing ovation.

Intrigued by the powerful connection that Abbé Pierre had made with the students, Dr. Brand asked one of them, "How did you understand the sermon since none of you speaks French?" The student replied, "We didn't need a language. We felt the presence of God and the presence of love."[8]

Abbé Pierre's unscripted sermon to medical students stands as a vivid image of preaching with incarnational presence. Pierre's personal presence communicated with his listeners in a way that transcended language. His message overflowed from the most deeply held convictions and passions of his heart. And, the result was more a spiritual experience than an educational program on the problems of homelessness. With no prior knowledge of Abbé Pierre and the story of his ministry, the students sensed his genuineness and wholehearted commitment. These elements of Pierre's spirit — passion, authenticity, boldness, overflowing love — became venues of God's presence through his personality. The student's comment, "We felt the presence of God and the presence of love," points to an incarnational moment in which God inhabited the lunchroom.

Incarnational presence is not a technique that one can practice or master by trying harder to be genuine in the pulpit. Preaching with

---

[8] Paul Brand and Philip Yancey, *Fearfully and Wonderfully Made* (Grand Rapids, MI: Zondervan, 1997), 54-55.

incarnational presence is more a spiritual posture than a skill set. Phillips Brooks wrote of the incarnational quality of presence in sermons, "Preaching is truth speaking through personality."[9] When the desire of the preacher is to be with God's people through the act of proclamation, the Word of God nestled in his heart becomes a living truth in the community. Time and again, I have witnessed the Word becoming flesh in Miller Chapel through the incarnational presence of David Sebastian.

One of the most meaningful experiences I have shared with Dr. Sebastian across the years was our partnership in crafting a preaching book I published under the title *The Poet-Gardener*. This work began as a dissertation for my doctoral work in pastoral preaching. Dr. Sebastian served as ordinarius in that process. As the compound metaphor, poet-gardener, suggests, I sought in this research to make a case for a model of preaching that inspires and nurtures. In the years since completing that project, I have come to see David Sebastian as a poet-gardener. He is one who brings great creativity and acumen to the task of preaching. And yet, there is something more. Dr. Sebastian models what it means to be a *poiema,* God's handiwork: "For we are God's handiwork, created in Christ Jesus to do good works, which God prepared in advance for us to do" (Ephesians 2:10, TNIV). Here is the "X" factor that has empowered this ordinary person to express his life vocation in such extraordinary ways as dean and preacher.

---

[9] Phillips Brooks, *The Joy of Preaching* (Grand Rapids, MI: Kregel, 1989), 29.

TEXTUAL AND CONTEXTUAL HERMENEUTICS

Gilbert Lozano

F irst of all, it is both a privilege and a joy to contribute this small article to someone who so well exemplifies the kind of approach that I identify with good hermeneutical practice. When David Sebastian preaches, one notices that he has spent considerable amounts of time poring over the biblical text. He is able to bring that text to life for his audience because of the care with which he approaches the text. This brief article is an homage to such a good interpreter and homiletician.

Christians claim that the Bible is the Word of God. Many think therefore that there is an immediate communication between God and the reader. Sometimes this is taken to extremes. A few years ago, some organization produced a new edition of the Bible that presumably was so easy to understand that the publishers felt confident to advertise it with the slogan "No interpretation needed." This claim sounds almost comical were it not for the fact that it does not do justice to the very nature of the Bible.

What is the Bible?

The Bible consists of a *collection* of ancient documents written in three languages over a period of a thousand years or more. No one today would claim that the English language has not changed in a thousand years or that *The Canterbury Tales* written by Chaucer in the 14th century require no interpretation. Something quite similar could be said of any of Shakespeare's works written in the early 1600s. If this is true of works written fairly recently in the English language, how could anyone claim that the language of the Bible transparently conveys a meaning that can be easily grasped by anyone regardless of background or the intellectual framework to deal with that ancient literature? The books contained in the Bible were written over a very long period of time in different places (Palestine, Babylonia, Persia, ancient Asia [now Turkey], Greece and probably even Rome). Moreover, the books were written by people from different cultural backgrounds — some were priests, others were court officials, others were simple individuals moved to write by religious convictions. To be sure, the Bible is united by a central unifying theme and thrust. It tells the story of God's dealing with a people and the effort to make that people live up to the divine promises — this is largely what scholars call the *history of salvation*. And yet, since antiquity, readers of the Bible have seen the enormous diversity of ideas found within its pages.

In sum, the Bible consists of dozens of books or documents written by many hands, over a very long period of time, and in different languages. Those facts alone should lead one to the conclusion that, in fact, interpretation is of the greatest importance.

Exegesis vs. Hermeneutics

The two terms are often misunderstood and conflated. Many people, especially Christians, see hermeneutics as the *application* of what one has found in the biblical text. Properly speaking, however, hermeneutics consists of the whole interpretive process, both exegesis and application. Moreover, exegesis refers to the art of extracting from a biblical passage what it may have meant in antiquity. To that end, interpreters of the Bible must first engage in the arduous process of eliciting, as much as possible, what the ancient meaning of the text may have been. Today the practitioners of this interpretive enterprise operate with the understanding that all of human discourse contains what Paul Ricoeur called "surplus of meaning"[1] and thus that it is possible to obtain multiple interpretations of the biblical text based largely on one's point

---

[1] Paul Ricoeur, *Interpretation Theory: Discourse and the Surplus of Meaning* (Fort Worth: Texas Christian University Press, 1976), 29-30, 45-47.

of departure, i.e., *my* specific context, or the place where I start, and the kinds of questions I bring to the text. In that regard, interpreters use a wide gamut of tools — from the traditional historical methodologies, such as textual, source, redaction, tradition, and form analysis, to newer methods, such as literary, rhetorical, social-scientific, and socially located methodologies.

Exegetical work is often invisible. It is akin to the roots of a tree, which cannot be seen. The deeper and stronger the roots (the exegetical work), the more robust the branches and limbs (interpretation) will be. Unfortunately, busy pastors often skip exegesis in favor of immediate interpretation, or they will rely on commentaries in order to move quickly to application because that is what their congregations expect. However, scholars and even noted homileticians and pastors have pointed out that the bulk of a pastor's study time should be spent doing exegesis. The fruits of that labor will be seen in healthy and sound preaching and teaching.

What Does Exegesis Look Like?

I have already pointed to the huge chasm that exists between ancient and contemporary readers of the Bible. How does one begin to bridge that chasm? I would suggest that one should approach the world of the Bible as one would approach any other cross-cultural experience. Reading the Bible is comparable to going on a cross-cultural trip to a foreign land. When you first land, you see that people are different: They speak a different language. They use bicycles as their primary means of transportation. They eat different foods than what you are used to eating. They do not practice Christianity, or any other form of religion to which you are accustomed. In fact, in close contact with the people you find out how vastly different their customs are from yours. Assuming you have no guide, a good place to start would be learning some of the language so that you can ask for directions and other things. Once you are able to form simple sentences, you can ask about the customs of the place, such as their traditions, their foods, and family habits, etc. Landing in this place and going straight to the business that you are interested in — for instance, the religious or cultural aspects of the place — would be impossible without first gaining some familiarity with the local language and customs, and becoming acquainted with the inhabitants. The more time you spend in this land and the more acquainted you become with the language and the customs, the better you will be able to understand what goes on in that culture and why people behave and think in the ways they do.

Similarly, biblical exegesis requires delving into the world of the people of the Bible. Here again, one is bound to encounter great diversity — first, the Bible begins telling the story of semi-nomads (Abraham and Sarah and their descendants) who sojourn from a distant land in Mesopotamia to the land of Canaan. The story continues in Egypt; from there it moves back to Canaan. The Israelites establish settled communities during the time of the monarchy. In that period, we witness the flourishing of the prophetic and wisdom traditions. Following the demise of the monarchies, the story of the Israelites shifts to the exiled communities in Babylon and Persia, and later to the dispersion of Jews living in many lands. And always the ancient Israelites are in close contact with the neighboring nations — both the local small nations of their vicinity, and the super powers of the time, Egypt, Assyria, Babylon, Persia, Greece and Rome.

From the foregoing we can conclude that the exegete must acquire some knowledge of Hebrew, Aramaic, and Greek, and must have the ability to use tools, such as concordances and Bible dictionaries, which define the usage of particular terms. The exegete must also read on the history and customs of the specific period in which the biblical passage on which he is working is likely to have been written and used.

Christian hermeneutics differs from many contemporary understandings due to its emphasis on application. We are not content with merely stating what a text meant in antiquity. In fact, that is not what hermeneutics means. In its best definition, hermeneutics is always interested in *translatio* (from Latin *trans* = across, over; and *latio* = carrying, bringing, rendering). In other words, hermeneutics is essentially the exercise of conveying (carrying over) to the contemporary listeners what the ancients heard.

The practical aspects of this are often referred to as the hermeneutic circle: we begin with our world — questions and problems that we are interested in solving — and since we are people of faith, we go to the Bible in order to ascertain what it may have to say about those issues. The next move is to bring those insights back into our contemporary world. These steps will be spelled out more fully in the next paragraphs.

Once the exegete has spent considerable time within the world of the ancient text, she then is ready to begin an exploration of the biblical text. Here, the exegete will ask questions like the five plus one journalistic W-questions: What, When, Where, Who, Why, and How? What kind of text is this (genre)? When and where was it written? Who wrote it and to whom? Why, or what prompted the writing of this text, and a related question, *how,* or under what circumstances was the text written? These questions should lead one to ask many other questions. The goal is to interrogate the text as a visitor interrogates a local in her foreign land. As Gerhard von Rad has proposed, "If in preaching on Old Testament texts the expositor wishes to find a rewarding and new point of departure, he must not shrink from becoming as familiar as possible with the character and nature of his text."[2] Once the exegete has asked and answered these questions from the text and its context, she can then begin to see how the particular text is structured in order to tackle the problem, issue, or task she has identified as the reason why the text was written in the first place.

Having spent much time on the text and its context, the exegete can take the next step in the interpretive process, namely, testing how that text may be applicable, or what it may have to say about her particular situation. It should be clear that one is not looking for exact correspondences because, as we have pointed out, there are vast differences between the ancient worlds of the Bible and our own. Of course, the validity of these approximations hinges on the work that the exegete has put into establishing the meaning of the ancient text and conversely reading her own context. This is not an easy task. In fact, because many preachers do not engage in this kind of exercise, they often force their own perceptions, aims and biases *into* the text. We call that *eisegesis* — bringing *into* the text, instead of leading *out*

---

[2] Gerhard von Rad, *Biblical Interpretations in Preaching* (transl. John E. Steely; Nashville, Abingdon, 1977), 40.

of the text (exegesis). We would do well to follow John Wesley's lead in this regard. Writing about his own methodology for teaching, he stated, "I apply no Scripture phrase either to myself or any other without carefully considering, both the *original* meaning and the *secondary* sense, wherein (allowing for different times and circumstances) it may be applied to ordinary Christians."[3]

What's more, a judicious practice of the exegetical process will show that direct application of the biblical text to a contemporary situation cannot be done. As I think will have become obvious by now, there are substantial differences between the ancient context and our own contexts. Therefore, there are no exact equivalences or one-to-one transpositions of meaning from the ancient world to our own. Rather, application requires also a complex reading and interpretation of our own situation in order to apply the insights one might have gained from reading the biblical text. In this regard, the exegete must keep an eye on the contemporary world. He must make an effort to understand the social, political, economic, and cultural dynamics that give rise to events in our own world. That requires interpretive skills similar to those one applies to any ancient context. That is to say, the exegete must *read* his context just like he reads any other context. Likewise, though it is now widely accepted that complete objectivity is unattainable, the exegete must make an effort to be as objective as possible, i.e., without passing judgment on either the contemporary or the ancient cultures. Keeping an open mind is a prerequisite for ascertaining the truth.

Moreover, as I suggested above, this process is described as a *hermeneutic circle* — i.e., it is never ending. Understanding hermeneutics as a circle or a spiral is realizing that change is a constant human dynamic: life and our individual contexts present ever new challenges and pose new questions that challenge people of faith to respond in new ways. If our situation changes, our understanding of the Bible also changes. In addition, the meaning of the Bible is illuminated by the insights brought up by biblical scholarship, which include better

---

[3] John Wesley, *The Methodist Societies: History, Nature, and Design.* The Works of John Wesley (ed. Rupert E. Davies; Nashville: Abingdon, 1989), 116.

understanding of the biblical languages and the customs and culture of people in antiquity. I am not suggesting that we adopt novelty for novelty's sake. Rather, I am proposing that interpreters be keenly aware of both the new demands of our culture and the new insights presented by biblical scholarship. The aim of this endeavor is to help us use the Bible responsibly in order to guide us toward Christian maturity. We call to mind the words of Old Testament scholar Brevard Childs who wrote, "[We understand] Scripture as a vehicle of a divine reality, which indeed encountered an ancient people in the historical past, but which continues to confront the church through the pages of Scripture."[4]

Finally, the approach that I am advocating for here is to a certain extent the development of the Wesleyan Quadrilateral. It consists of the use of four elements — Scripture, tradition, reason and experience — in order to respond adequately to the issues that confront us. While Wesley recognized the primacy of Scripture, he was also aware that Christians are heirs of, and often interpret the Bible by way of, tradition. Likewise, since God has endowed us with thinking capacities and we recognize the advancement of human knowledge, we must also use reason. Lastly, our *experience* both as individuals and as member of human communities is a valid instrument as well. Truth is to be found at the intersection of these four sources or authorities, which are ever present in our lives.

All of our interpretive work is done in the awareness that God is actively operating towards the redemption of the world. As Walter Brueggemann has pointed out, "It is, of course, impossible to tell this story without the defining agency of YHWH who is decisive in every point of the story... There is no story without the character of YHWH."[5]

---

[4] Brevard Childs, *Biblical Theology in Crisis* (Philadelphia: Westminster Press, 1970), 100.

[5] Walter Brueggemann, *The Practice of Prophetic Imagination: Preaching an Emancipating Word* (Minneapolis: Fortress, 2012), 13.

PREACHING AND FINDING YOUR VOICE

Kimberly S. Majeski

I t beats inside our hearts, a rhythm like the rush of a rolling river. The thrum and hum of words whirl and turn inside, attach themselves to images that are long held and known like the crevices of our own hand; the river is true and deep and wide. As children we sat at the feet of storytellers and saints, and the ancient narratives caught our hearts. Seeds planted and watered were nurtured to grow. We stood with Miriam in the reeds watching over the baby in the basket beside the shimmering cerulean Nile. We sat beneath the palm trees, feet soaked in sun and sand, and we heard the cries of our children, settled land disputes, and listened for God's call on the wind, holding hands with Deborah, prophet and judge of Yahweh's unfaithful bride. We knew a spiritual kindred, an eternal bond with Mary, this woman child who birthed forth the Word; we knew her, felt her heart, sensed her pain somewhere hidden and true. It is from this river that every preacher must draw, must reach down deep into that well of what she knows, into that current that is at the heart of her becoming to cradle the stories that have been her song, to find her own voice, to know her own vessel unto the proclamation of good news.

The pilgrimage of voice is a paramount process for every preacher. The labor of discovering one's own unique timbre lives somewhere beyond the work of exegesis and the historical critical method, far out past manuscript variations, textual and syntactical issues, at the end of Hebrew translation and reception history. On the edge of study and before the birth of proclamation lies the sacred task of giving voice to biblical truth, to emanate words from one's own story for the good of the community of faith assembled. Those who would prepare, then, for the vocation of ministry, for the office of preacher, must do more than learn to mine the Christian texts and holy books. Those whose lives will be given as heralds of *kerygma* will also need to mine their own lives. Those who are called to the daunting task of preaching must not only be well versed in biblical languages, church history, and cultural relevancy, but must also find some confidence in their own unique voice so that the texts and the process must first incarnate the preacher before she might inform and challenge and shape the community.

Perhaps we are helped to discuss here the process, the labyrinth from discovery to pronouncement as a series of movements. Some years ago, Andy Stanley and Lane Jones authored a book, *Communicating for Change,* in which they outlined a helpful process for those learning the art of public speaking. Stanley and Jones suggest a pattern of "Me-We-God-You-We" as the basic road map for effective communication.[1] For them, the idea is that speakers would craft their material around the ideas above so that the calculated progression of the talk would build towards a climax through the notion of a natural flow of conversation. While Stanley and Jones offer a helpful guide, this essay will tweak the process and suggest some changes to reflect the particularity of sermon craft for the building up of the Kingdom of God. Here the discovery of voice is fashioned around the art of story such that the sermon then is crafted from Spirit revelation in God's story as well as in our own.

Our Story

The beginning of a sermon intended for the community of the baptized is always the collective human experience. Quite naturally, as we want to draw those assembled into our conversation, into the experience of the Gospel enacted, we begin by building connection. In *Blue Like Jazz: Non-Religious Thoughts on Faith,* Donald Miller reminds us that people only really listen to the folks they believe genuinely like them.[2] Miller's point instructs us to remember that in our

---

[1] Andy Stanley and Lane Jones, *Communicating for Change: Seven Keys to Irresistible Communication* (Colorado Springs: Multnomah Books, 2006), 46.

[2] Donald Miller, *Blue Like Jazz: Non-Religious Thoughts on Faith* (Nashville: Thomas Nelson, 2003), 222.

first moments of proclamation it is crucial that we connect, bond, forge relationship with the listener so that our teaching, our exposition, our truth will be received.

To be sure, this is an important first step in the dynamic relationship of preacher and congregation established in the initial moments of the preaching act, and it is here that many well-intentioned preachers fail to relate to their hearers. This is where a pastor must know intimately her community, must understand the journey they are on together, must be aware of the struggles and losses and celebrations that together weave the story of those who have assembled. Here we reflect on the words of William Willimon, who suggests that pastors should understand worship as pastoral care; the question before each preacher is, "How can I help my congregation do what they want to do (worship God) but may not remember how to do?"[3] This becomes more difficult, of course, if the preacher is visiting or is not known to the congregation. In this case, the preacher must be aware of universal needs, conversations that are national and local so that she might engage those who have come to worship. Whatever the context, some common thread must be found and spoken forth so that preacher and congregation hold hands and place trust in one another as together they move forward in the experience.

In this task, we are instructed by the example of the Apostle Paul, who was, in every sense of the word, a relational leader. For Paul, it was critical to situate himself within the community so that he might speak to it. Paul was not only a student of Hebrew Scriptures, but he was also well versed in the philosophies of Greek culture and Roman religious practices of the day. He was able to know and be known in the communities in which he preached, such that after he departed he could write back to them and address specific community concerns. Though there are more examples than space will allow, consider his expert approach in Galatians where at once he is addressing the Celts of Galatia and the Judaizers from Antioch and knows so intimately the debates among them that he is able to thwart both at the same time.

In chapter 3, he masterfully scolds the Galatians and discusses salvation in terms of circumcision, which is the matter at issue, while

---

[3] William Willimon, *Worship as Pastoral Care* (Nashville: Abingdon, 1979), 18.

relating stories of Abraham and interpreting the circumcision act now a matter of heart (3:1-29).

God's Story

Once a connection has been established, the preacher can move to relating God's story to the congregation. This is perhaps the *sweet spot* for those who have labored over texts and word studies, who have spent long years in seminary and ministry preparation, who have dug out the truth of the scriptures and the white spaces in between for the good of the church. It is tempting then, for an equipped and ordained preacher to unload all her knowledge in one sermon at one place in time, and preachers who fall prey to this temptation quickly lose their connection to the people they have stood forward to encourage. The suggestion here is not that the study be negated or the methods of exegesis not applied. On the contrary, arduous study and the deep work of parsing ancient texts is a must; however, the preacher must distill this information, must evaluate what portions help illuminate the message, must decide which points help her tell God's story to the church.

Consider for a moment some of the miraculous, fantastic, life-changing stories of Hebrew and Christian scripture. Recall God's wedding God's self to Abraham in Genesis 15. Remember Lot's daughters seducing their own father after the destruction of Sodom and Gomorrah (Gen. 19:30-38), God's moving in to kill Moses on the way down to Egypt because Moses' son had not yet been circumcised (Ex. 4:24-26), Jesus' revolutionary claim that he would be found in the least of these (Matthew 25:31-46), Mary of Migdol's history-altering role as first herald of the resurrection (John 20:1-18), Paul's gratitude to Prisca and Aquilla for "risking their necks" for his life (Romans 16:3,4). The narratives of scripture are rich and potent and human — such that our sermons should invite listeners into the struggle, allow them to get their hands dirty, to taste and smell the bread and wine, to hear the wind rustle in the silvery leaves of the olive tree, and to feel the salt spray of the Mediterranean on their sun-splotched cheeks. Likewise, preachers should draw from the deep well of inspired texts instead of moving instantly to draw spiritual platitudes in effort to domesticate ancient stories that are wild and free. When we relay the story of Jesus' walking on the water, it seems ill informed to move to the application of Jesus' ability to calm the stormy seas of life. Rather, we should relay the power and supernatural wonder of the miraculous claim that *Jesus walked on the water* (Matt. 14:22,23).

My Story

Once the preacher has drawn the listener in, bonded over some deep knowing, and has allowed the narrative of scripture to rattle the cages of hearts and minds, the preacher should then move to the moment of revelation when she makes known how her own heart and mind have been moved by the Spirit's work in this text. Too often preachers err on one side of this path or the other as some use the entire time reflecting on one's own experience, or the preacher is uncomfortable baring herself, allowing her own struggle to be seen, so she is closed off from experiencing the enactment of the story that she heralds. Ronald Sleeth suggests that many preachers are afraid of the preaching office because it reveals their own interior life and this seems threatening.[4]

This movement, too, is critical in the preaching act. It is here that the preacher invites the listener in, steps down from the lofty place, and bares her own dirty feet. It is at this point that the gathered community begins to understand their preacher is no different than they. It is here that we remember as the family of God why we have come together in the first place, because life is hard and sometimes God doesn't seem to make sense and, we need each other to speak truth and reality. We do not gather together because we are righteous. We gather together because we are broken and bruised and in need of words of life. Here the preacher gives voice to how the story of God has found her and made her new. Here the preacher tells the truth about her own broken self and relays the Gospel medicine: broken people need each other to find their way through.

---

[4] Ronald Eugene Sleeth, "Crisis in Teaching," *Perkin's Journal* 30 no. 4 (June 1977), 1-41.

Your Story

Once the preacher has authentically poured forth her own self, she is ready now to ask her listeners to look to their own selves. It is only once the preacher has opened her own story that she is allowed to ask the congregation to do the same. Since the preacher has been transparent, since she has risked through the liturgical relationship of the preaching act, she is now able to invite the congregation to follow her lead. Now, the community who has been holding hands with her since the beginning, who has opened themselves to hear the ground-shaking, life-changing, preconceived-notion-shattering message of the good news, receives her in her own frailty before the truth and is now safe to permit this preacher to lead them to look inside themselves and ask the hard questions of the text. It is when we do this together that we become family, we become one. Barbara Brown Taylor puts it this way, "Coming together for worship, individuals may release their fragile hold on 'my truth' for an hour or two in order to explore the time-traveling, ego-rattling, neighbor-loving dimensions of 'our truth' instead."[5] Brown Taylor adds that anyone who's ever been a part of a congregation knows this is more about being one body than one mind.[6]

Conclusion

What can be seen here is that the preacher's own pilgrimage becomes an invitation for her congregation. It is in finding her own voice that she is then able to extend a hand towards the community and invite them to do the same along with her. The search for voice in preaching then, is not only process and property of the preacher, rather, it becomes the binding feature of the congregation who has decided to be present, to be awake, to be open to hear what the Spirit is saying to the church.

---

[5] Barbara Brown Taylor, "Telling Truths," *Christian Century,* 123 no. 15 (July 2006), 31.

[6] Ibid.

EVANGELISM

"They Will Know Us by Our Love": "Good News" in a Postmodern, Postcolonial, Post-Christian Context

Cassie J. E. H. Trentaz

C an I be honest? When I hear the word "evangelism," it makes my brow furrow. It comes as a reflex. I simply don't feel comfortable using the word. It feels clumsy to me in my 21st century "postmodern"/"postcolonial"/"post-Christian" U.S. context. It feels ill-fitting, like I'm dressing up in someone else's far-too-big and far-too-baggy clothes. Or, perhaps more accurately, it feels like the clothes are far too tight or constricting in all the wrong places (like lacy elastic wrist cuffs, perhaps, to access an unpleasant childhood memory). The word "evangelism" is not a part of my regular vernacular. It has history. Some of that history comes with complicated baggage for someone like me. I'm quite sure that I'm not alone.

All of that may sound strange coming from a faith tradition that affirms and promotes the call to spread the "good news" to everyone in the world, a tradition that in fact affirms and promotes that that good news is, indeed, accessible and for everyone in the world. This is a piece that I love about our Wesleyan-Holiness roots, which brings me back to my point — perhaps it's inappropriate. It certainly is not the whole or perhaps not even the "majority" story, but when I hear the word "evangelism" in my context and through my lenses as a postmodern/ postcolonial theo-ethicist trained and rooted in liberation struggles and contextual details of how our ideas of God are shaped by and in turn shape our real, embodied, concrete, historic, geo-cultural contexts, it conjures images of colonial/imperial expansionism, appeals to authority perhaps disconnected to real stories and their implications, tendencies to ignore or dismiss physical or material conditions of one's life, and how the church may have even been complicit in creating or supporting the conditions where some are consistently hungry and others have excess to waste at the end of the day (deep breath). In these local and global conditions, good news is absolutely necessary. But I flinch at the word "evangelism." It's a word that has sometimes accompanied postures that dismiss key components of human experience, and, therefore, key populations of neighbors needing actual good news.

If you want to spark passion and fire, however, if you want me to explore something that I can give my life to fully, let's talk about love. And if you want to explore the enduring claims of Christianity from the place where I stand and work and live and the ears through which I hear, informed by the experiences of those often held without voice in the history of global Christianity, let's talk about what I have come to call "the five loves" that sit at the heart of the Christian message — the love of God, self, neighbor, "enemy," and world. This is what life is about. This is what it looks like to follow Jesus. Wait — what is the role of love in evangelism? Perhaps that's exactly the reason for us to look at this tricky word and practice anew in our time and in our places.

It likely comes as no surprise to any of us that none of this started with us. We are a part of the wide family of religious traditions, commitments, and expressions known as Christianity. According to communal memory, these traditions, although holding diverse interpretations of what it means, arose from a community gathered around a central figure: Jesus — a lower-economic, colonized, Palestinian Jew. And according to the communal memory and our central text, the biblical canon, we find a story of someone coming to this central figure (Jesus) and asking him, "What is central?" The good news is, as the story goes, he responded and did so by giving us what we now know as the great commandments: love God with everything you are and have and, in so doing, love your neighbor and/as yourself. Everything hinges upon these loves. And if we read the notion of "neighbor" through the lens of the rest of the canon, we see also the call for Christ-followers to love our so-called enemies (our not-yet-recognized-as-neighbors) and the world (our eco-neighbors). We might call these five loves the "kingdom" or "kin-dom" method or the path to "shalom" or that reality when "all will be well."

Each group since has had the responsibility to ask the questions of what it means to be faithful, responsible lovers "here" and "now." Our particular roots stem from a movement in the late 1800s that looked at the results of colonization, burgeoning industrialization, and rise of urbanization and said "wait — there are folks on the streets becoming poorer, sicker, and exhausted and folks in the churches are getting comfortable and disconnected from that reality and from each other. Where is love in this? Where is one-ness in this? What does it mean to be faithful and responsible real lovers in these contexts?" That movement, which gave birth to the Church of God, understood the basics of love through two loaded words — holiness and unity. ("Yeah, yeah, yeah," you might be saying. "We know all of this already, so what does it have to do with evangelism in a 'postmodern context?'" We're getting there.)

What our movement has been saying, importantly, for generations now in articulating the vitality of holiness for the Christ-follower is that our behaviors matter. How we use our resources and treat ourselves, each other, and the earth matters. And, because we are a part of a tradition that's a particular kind of holiness — a Wesleyan-Holiness — we assert a "social holiness." This is not primarily an isolated, protective "I don't drink, smoke or chew or go with girls who do" holiness. It's a holiness that says we are not holy if we are not ever-increasing in love for God, self, neighbor, enemy, and world. And love is not love if it's not practical, rooted in the contexts of those with need, and directly addressing that need toward the creation of the Kingdom/Kin-dom of the God who loves in the world. We're a part of a people who said that our holiness actually depends on, is defined by this ever-increasing love of God, self, neighbor, enemy, and world. As such, our goal is not to remain "clean," unafraid to touch the "unclean" for fear of becoming "unclean" ourselves, but we hold to the stories of Jesus who had the courage to be and be with the "unclean" hoping that together we might create "a new clean." As such, our goal is also not just to address the needs of one's soul but those of the entire person (and community). That's who we are. Our behaviors in the world matter and we know it. We want others to recognize it, too. And we are empowered and responsible to participate with God in the creation of the "all will be well" in the world.

We're also a part of a people who recognized that we are neither alone in the world nor self-sufficient in this. We need each other and there is something holy about leaning on one another in being the image of the communal (Trinitarian) and incarnate (embodied in time and place) God whom we love and who loves us and calls us to love. There is something revolutionary in modeling interconnectedness, mutuality, communality among cultural threads that lean toward individualism, self-sufficiency, competition. We are a part of a people who recognized that being with others is actually an essential component to living a life ever-increasing in love and that lines that intentionally divide destroy the one-ness of the body of Christ in the world. Our one-ness, our being-with one another, our resistance of "us" and "them" toward only "us" is proof of our Christ-following. We cannot love what we do not know and we cannot know what we don't make time and space to hear and learn.

Here's an example. Sometimes our entire department gathers for meals. We have a particular student currently in the department who has a gluten intolerance. She simply can't eat some things without them making her sick. If I didn't know that, the offerings of food that I would bring out of love for my students would make my student sick. I had to get to know her before I could know what communicates as real love. What's more, this particular student is used to bringing her own food so as not to "be too much trouble" in order to be a part of the group. Our practice of intentionally providing food that our student can eat communicates that she is part of us. Her presence is important. Making adjustments is not a "bother" but an act of welcome and love. We want her with us unashamedly. The good news in this example is material, practical, and rooted in a knowing relationship.

This is part of unity. It's not an amorphous unity that discounts the value of each unique person. The love of each "self" is affirmed and balanced with the love of each "other." We're part of a people who looked around and said, "Why are some of our neighbors missing from the table? Are they exhausted? Voiceless? We're not complete without them." That's who we are.

But our goal is not togetherness alone. It's a particular type we call the Kingdom or Kin-dom of God. This is not for another time and place but has real implications and expectations for our real decisions and our real participation here and now. It's not solely a spiritual kin-dom but a body and soul kin-dom — a kin-dom of enough bread for hungry bellies as well as salvation for hungry souls. It's not an exclusive and protective kin-dom but an inclusive kin-dom of just peace — of love for even our enemies with a big enough table where all know themselves loved and can know and love themselves and neighbors and, in so doing, God. That's what we work for. That sounds like good news — not simply proclaimed but enacted and sometimes over a long haul, with a long view, stretching across generations in hope.

My initial confession opening this chapter indicates where perhaps we've been off kilter. Some of us have too often heard and seen folks who seem only concerned with our spiritual health, while leaving our bellies hungry for material bread, those who are content in a lifestyle marked by economic, political, and spiritual "security" and "freedom" but who don't seem to recognize that I cannot hear a message of good news that does not address what kind of news would actually sound/be received as "good" in the concrete, practical conditions of my everyday living here and now. Some of us have heard messages of "love" from those who do not even know us and seem perhaps not to care to know us. This is why my furrowed brow.

This is a problem. "Postmodern"/"postcolonial"/"post-Christian" Christianity needs to recognize and reckon with a posture of cultural distrust for "evangelists." First, culturally, we have a bit of an authority problem. This is nothing new, but it has been brewing in different forms for generations if not for all time. Second, we don't feel heard. We don't trust someone who doesn't listen to us. Why would we? Don't pretend to love me if you don't take time to know me. And, third, many of us don't see evangelists in our communities as those who are living particularly meaningful, fully alive lives of love, joy, peace, patience, kindness, goodness, faithfulness, gentleness, and self-control. We often see fear, divisiveness, insecurity, and inability to trust that they are loved, which prevent them from thoughtfully loving us in return. That's something to lament. It doesn't have to be this way.

For some of us, the "good news" has been boiled down to a formula. We don't want a formula. We don't want flashy slogans or billboards or sound bites. We want thickness, rootedness, something textured and that's big enough to be worthy of a whole life. We want stories of what holds believers together. We want to be connected to the big story that spans generations. We want to see the fruits in the life of the messenger and in his or her method. We want news that is good in the midst of our real lives and the questions that emerge within them. We want someone who is willing to kneel next to us and doodle in the dust for awhile, even if in silence, even while others stand ready with stones, not dismissing or condemning, but being-with until the chaos settles down.

Living a Christ-like life is more than "saying the prayer" and being cool when it comes to heaven. It effects real changes in real conditions in real, historic, embodied, geographical, cultural contexts. This is where I think the Church of God (Anderson, IN) has something so beautiful still to offer — we know that our behaviors matter and we know that we are interconnected. We come from a tradition that says God cares about both body and soul, health and holiness, and that humans can (and are expected to) participate with God in the care for each other, ourselves, and the world. We are empowered and expected to participate in the work now. We each have something meaningful to contribute to the whole in the journey toward its "all being well." That's good news. And, we're also not alone — it's not wholly dependent upon us. That's good news, too.

Evangelism, to be good news in the 21st century, means that "they will know that we are Christians by our love." When we love deeply, we are participating in the process of sharing good news in the world. Evangelism, to be received as good news in the 21st century, means to be converted to our neighbor not as a soul needing to be saved but in awe at the wonder that she or he is with intrinsic value to God and to the world. Then, receiving the gift of one another, it means we are mutually converted to the continued process of ever-increasing in love for God, ourselves, each other, and the world. This brings us to the responsibility to resist boiling things down too much and to ask ourselves thoughtfully, what are the markers of love? How do we know it when we see it or experience it? How do we recognize it when it has been received as love by another? How do we cultivate love in the real world?

Someone once venturing a response to those questions asserted that love is patient and kind. It does not envy or boast. It is not proud. It is not rude or self-seeking. It is not easily angered. It does not dwell on and keeps no record of wrongs. Love does not delight in evil but rejoices with the truth. It always protects, always trusts, always hopes, always perseveres. Perhaps that, too, is the essence of evangelism with real effect in the 21st century.

URBAN EVANGELISM

Kevin Early

D avid Sebastian supplies a working definition of evangelism in his book *Recovering Our Nerve:*

> Evangelism is communicating in word and deed the liberating power of the gospel and, through the guidance of the Holy Spirit, inviting people to repent of sin, to be baptized in the name of the triune God, confessing Jesus as Savior and Lord, and to be incorporated into the church as the visible expression of the kingdom of God in this age and the age to come.[1]

With all the hardship, poverty, political corruption, sinfulness, and distrust of organized religion that is so often present in urban settings, why would Christians endeavor to evangelize in an urban context? Why assume the risk? Why address or attempt to minister to the unchurched when they may end up insulted or offended? Why not simply form a holy community that seeks God and sticks to itself? As I think about these questions and topic of urban evangelism the following words of Paul come to mind:

> Cheerfully pleasing God is the main thing, and that's what we aim to do, regardless of our conditions. Sooner or later we'll all have to face God, regardless of our conditions. We will appear before Christ and take what's coming to us as a result of our actions, either good or bad.
>
> That keeps us vigilant, you can be sure. It's no light thing to

---

[1] David Sebastian, *Recovering Our Nerve: A Primer for Evangelism in Everyday Life* (Anderson, IN: Warner Press, 2013), 9-10.

know that we'll all one day stand in that place of judgment. That's why we work urgently with everyone we meet to get them ready to face God. God alone knows how well we do this, but I hope you realize how much and deeply we care. We're not saying this to make ourselves look good to you. We just thought it would make you feel good, proud even, that we're on your side and not just nice to your face as so many people are. If I acted crazy, I did it for God; if I acted overly serious, I did it for you. Christ's love has moved me to such extremes. His love has the first and last word in everything we do.

Our firm decision is to work from this focused center: One man died for everyone. That puts everyone in the same boat. He included everyone in his death so that everyone could also be included in his life, a resurrection life, a far better life than people ever lived on their own.

Because of this decision, we don't evaluate people by what they have or how they look. We looked at the Messiah that way once and got it all wrong, as you know. We certainly don't look at him that way anymore. Now we look inside, and what we see is that anyone united with the Messiah gets a fresh start, is created new. The old life is gone; a new life burgeons! Look at it! All this comes from the God who settled the relationship between us and him, and then called us to settle our relationships with each other. God put the world square with himself through the Messiah, giving the world a fresh start by offering forgiveness of sins. God has given us the task of telling everyone what he is doing. We're Christ's representatives. God uses us to persuade men and women to drop their differences and enter into God's work of making things right between them. We're speaking for Christ himself now: Become friends with God; he's already a friend with you (2 Corinthians 5:9-20, MSG).

As I reflect on this scripture, I draw four conclusions that lend answers to the aforementioned questions. These conclusions form a foundation for urban evangelism, coupled with Christ's instructions in the Great Commission, "All authority in heaven and on earth has been given to me. Therefore go and make disciples of all nations, baptizing them in the name of the Father and of the Son and of the Holy Spirit, and teaching them to obey everything I have commanded you. And surely I am with you always, to the very end of the age" (Matthew 28:18-20, NIV).

First, Christians should work to evangelize spurred by a fear of the Righteous Judge. In essence, Paul describes himself as being guided by the fear of the Lord as he endeavors to persuade others of the gospel of Jesus Christ. While some Scriptures use the phrase "fear of the Lord" to refer to reverence, awe, and respect, fear in this text goes beyond reverence, awe, and respect to actual apprehension. In other words, Paul is referring to a strong desire to avoid punishment for disobedient inaction.

This reminds me of the occasional Saturday morning fear I had growing up when my mother told me to have the kitchen cleaned before she returned home. I did not know if she would be back quickly or take a long time, but I surely did not want to face the consequences of her returning home before I had cleaned the kitchen. Consequently, I would forsake what I wanted to do with my time at the moment and clean the kitchen. Similarly, a proper fear of displeasing the Righteous Judge can help us overcome the fear of rejection when we engage in evangelistic endeavors in urban contexts and motivate us to do what we have been commissioned by Christ to do.

Second, the love that Christ has for us ought to compel his followers to evangelize the unchurched. A Christian has been adopted into the family of God, forgiven of their sins, saved from an eternity of torment, freed from selfish pursuits, given newness of life, blessed with a heavenly King, and promised the provision of all their needs — all of which evidences God's love for them. Therefore, when a disciple of Christ examines what God has done collectively and individually for the redeemed and allows the action of God to glide on their consciousness it will motivate them to answer Christ's call to join him in his mission of establishing his kingdom in our nation's urban and rural areas.

Third, disciples of Christ should find themselves engaged in urban evangelism as a result of being convinced of the value of every person for whom Jesus Christ died and was raised to redeem. This truth is particularly relevant in urban settings that are full of diversity. In order to evangelize effectively in an urban setting, members of the body of Christ must be comfortable ministering to every human in whom Christ desires to reign. To be specific, this includes women and men; girls and boys; Black, White, Hispanic, Arab, and Caucasian; rich and poor; people from the suburbs and those living in less affluent neighborhoods; people blessed with jobs and those who rely on welfare; heterosexual, homosexual, and bi-sexual; people who are young and those who are formerly young; people free from criminal history and felons; people with low self-esteem and the conceited; gossipers and the tight-lipped — the list could go on and on.

Growing up I had a baseball card collection. One of the valued tools of my trade was a book that indicated the value of each baseball card. I would later learn that the value of each baseball card was not really found in the book but in the price someone else was willing to pay me for a specific baseball card. If I found someone willing to pay only $5 for a baseball card otherwise listed as $20, for my purposes the value was $5. The inverse was also true. In the same way, the fact that Jesus shed his invaluable blood to cover every sinner's stains, serves as evidence that each and every person, regardless of the demographic categories that they fit into, has substantial value. Valuable people need to hear and experience the priceless gospel of Jesus Christ.

Fourth, endeavoring to evangelize the unchurched is not optional because every citizen of God's Kingdom is given the task of representing Christ and spreading his gospel message. Moreover, the appropriate response and celebration of our reconciliation, our restored relationship with the Father, is to share the good news of hope and reconciliation with other people. Darryl B. Starnes Sr. comments,

> There is no doubt that the Apostle Paul saw evangelism as a way of life. For him new life in Christ meant more than simply enjoying the benefits of reconciliation with God. It meant becoming an ambassador for Christ, entrusted with the ministry

and the message of reconciliation. It meant a lifelong ministry of compelling people to be reconciled to God through Jesus Christ.[2]

A believer's belief and confession of the four conclusions will not automatically yield a fruitful harvest for the Kingdom in urban settings. In fact, if there is ever a location that requires a Christian's beliefs and convictions to lead to tangible action, it is in the urban setting. As James so aptly notes, "faith by itself, if it is not accompanied by action, is dead" (James 2:17). Moreover, when faith leads to evangelistic work in an urban setting, the church's influence reaches beyond its building and into the dark world that so desperately needs the power of the gospel.

As congregation members commit to express their belief and convictions through evangelism, it is important for them to resist the temptation of labeling prayer, righteous living, and inviting people to church as evangelism. While these three things are significant, they do not equate to or serve as substitutes for evangelism. Of course, prayer is vitally important in the overall effort to establish the Kingdom of God in the hearts of women and men, but prayer absent actual word and deeds will not lead to disciples being made, especially in light of the fact that "faith comes from hearing the message, and the message is heard through the word about Christ" (Romans 10:17). Churches can fast and pray, but if they do not actually reach out and evangelize people in their community, they will not experience heaven's rule in their hearts. Similarly, a righteous life lived before non-believers is important, but if Christ is never revealed as the source and sustainer of one's righteous life, the unchurched are less likely to inquire, "How can I be saved?" Inviting the unchurched to attend Christian worship services is admirable, but again, it should not be confused with evangelism. In other words, an invitation to church and an invitation to the Lordship of Christ are not synonymous. Moreover, urban evangelism requires a willingness to go where the unchurched are located.

---

[2] Darryl B. Starnes, Sr., *Equipping the Saints for the Work of Ministry: Teaching Adults to Share Their Faith at Evans Metropolitan African Methodist Episcopal Zion Church, Bennettsville, South Carolina.* D.Min diss., Samford University Beeson Divinity School, 1998.

Convinced of our call to evangelize and having an awareness of activities that are not synonymous with evangelism, what avenue can Christians use to evangelize practically and effectively in urban settings? I suggest that one of the more powerfully effective ways is to have members of the body engage in direct conversations with non-believers. A major opportunity for evangelism in an urban setting is for Christians to have direct conversations with people they already have relationships with and people they do not know whom they intentionally reach out to and converse with. Put another way, in an urban setting Christians should strive and be encouraged to evangelize their neighbors, co-workers, classmates, family, friends, and others with whom they have meaningful or casual relationships. Urban settings also provide an abundance of opportunity to evangelize in malls, grocery stores, airports, restaurants, coffee shops, barbershops, parades, parties, sporting events, bars, and literally anywhere that the unchurched might gather.

As I pastor the Metropolitan Church of God in Detroit, I encourage the members to have evangelistic conversations that plant seeds, water seeds, or reap spiritual harvest. In my observation,

> we plant seeds when we articulate gospel truths to nonbelievers, introducing it into their hearts. If we invite our listeners to become disciples of Jesus at this point, we are likely to be rejected. We water seeds when we reaffirm the truth that has already been planted in their hearts. Once again, our nonbelieving friends may not choose to follow Jesus. When a Christian reaps a spiritual harvest, the nonbeliever accepts the invitation to discipleship, experiences rebirth, and begins a lifelong journey with Jesus as his or her Lord. It should be noted that when a Christian starts an evangelistic conversation with a nonbeliever, they may not know whether they will plant, water, or reap a spiritual harvest, although the gospel truth they share is exactly the same."[3]

In order to strengthen the fruitfulness of evangelistic conversations

---

[3] Kevin W. Earley, *Every-Member Ministry: Spiritual Gifts and God's Design For Service.* (Anderson, IN: Warner Press, 2013), 36-37.

in an urban setting, deliberate measures must be taken to teach members how to start, conduct, and end evangelistic conversations. Growing up in Chicago, the Church of God congregations I was a part of taught us how to attempt soul-winning using what is often referred to as the Roman Road to Salvation, which is "a selection of Bible verses taken from the book of Romans that present the plan of salvation through faith in Jesus Christ."[4] Unfortunately, I was never given practical methods to have conversations at the school lunch table or in my high school baseball locker room.

As I spoke with the members of Metropolitan, I learned that the majority thoroughly believed in evangelizing, were convinced of its necessity, understood the Roman Road, but did not actually attempt to lead others to Christ because they lacked the practical tools and skills to begin, conduct, and end evangelistic conversations. I also discovered that once the members developed and strengthened the tools and skills necessary, they were willing and even excited about having evangelistic conversations with people they had relationships with and those they had just met.

Consequently, effective urban evangelism requires that church members develop entries into evangelistic conversations. Three entries I have found to be effect are, (A) "I have been working on a project and surveying people. May I ask you a question? What do you believe happens to people when they die?" (B) "Given (a recent local, national, or international calamity), what do you believe happened to the people after they died?" (C) "People tend to have significant meanings behind their tattoos, will you share the story behind yours with me?" Quite often the stories behind tattoos deal with grief or significant life events, supplying ideal opportunities to talk about faith.

After genuinely listening to a person's response, being able to summarize the content of their response correctly and refusing to be combative frequently provides an opportunity for a believer to plant seeds, water seeds, or reap a spiritual harvest. Based on how the

---

[4] Teen Mission International, "Roman Road to Salvation," http://www. teenmissions.org/resources/roman-road-to-salvation/ (accessed March 10, 2014.)

conversation transpires and the guidance of the Holy Spirit, the church member may or may not seek a decision for Christ, having a comfort and trust that they can end the conversation and let the Lord finish what he has started through them at the appropriate time. Put another way, successful evangelism will not always end in rebirth or a "repeat after me" prayer.

Another important component of preparing members of the body for evangelistic conversations is to prepare them for common responses and objections. While I thoroughly disagree with their stance on Jesus Christ, I do admire how Jehovah's Witnesses seem to be prepared at every corner for the objections to their message. Similarly, those who embrace the truth of Jesus Christ should be prepared for common responses and objections. An example of a common response is the incorrect notion that as long as a person's good outweighs their bad they will get into heaven. A Christian being prepared to ask, "What if you are not right?" may very well alter another person's eternity. Mark Cahill in his book *One Thing You Can't Do In Heaven* provides invaluable entries, thoughtful responses to common objections, and useful approaches for handing out gospel tracts.[6]

In addition to being prepared with thoughtful responses to common objections to Christianity, in an urban setting it is also helpful for members to learn how to ask questions that allow unchurched individuals to reach the right conclusions as opposed to telling them what to believe. This is particularly important in current urban areas because, "Many postmoderns and many who are not connected to the church or faith are much more responsive to the 'asking questions' model of coaching then the 'telling' posture of traditional teaching."[6] Cahill explains, "Finding out what people believe, and why they believe it, is essential in a good witnessing situation. Keep in mind that you don't have to do all the proving in a conversation. Ask non-believers to

---

[5] For more information about Mark Cahill and his evangelistic resources, visit www.markcahill.org.

[6] Edward H. Hammet and James R. Pierce, *Reaching People Under 40 While Keeping People Over 60* (St. Louis, MO: Chalice Press, 2007), 131.

try to prove their positions on eternity and God."[7] I have witnessed how asking questions can raise doubt in an atheist's mind about their beliefs more efficiently than simply explaining that they have an incorrect belief system.

A final suggestion for strengthening evangelistic conversations is for church members to engage in role plays and prepare and examine verbatims. During role plays, church members practice their evangelistic skills on one another before using their techniques in the real world. This allows those who participate and those who listen to learn and build their repertoire of responses. Another practical tool that the members of my congregation have found useful is verbatims, wherein a church member writes down, line-by-line, the evangelistic conversation they had with a non-believer to the best of their ability. The script is then shared with the evangelism class for critique and reflection. This gives the person who wrote the verbatim an opportunity to reflect on what was said, what could have been said, and what should not have been said. Overall, it provides everyone in the class an opportunity to learn from each other's successful and questionable responses.

In a verbatim I prepared for a class, I shared a jovial response someone gave me that really stumped me in the moment, leaving me in the position of not knowing what to say. After further reflection and discussion, the members of the class and I hope someone gives a similar response in the future, because we will all be well prepared to respond. After I led members of my congregation through an evangelism class that included role playing and verbatims, they went on to be very comfortable and successful engaging people they met for the first time in a local grocery store while taking their final exam. A host of students have also reported their increased level of comfort initiating conversations with their family, friends, and co-workers as a result of our role plays and verbatims.

As believers accept God's call to make disciples and prepare themselves to do so, not only will they please the Lord, they will make a spiritual difference in the lives of others now and for all eternity.

---

[7] Mark Cahill, *One Thing You Can't Do In Heaven* (Rockwall, TX: Biblical Discipleship Publishers, 2002-20011), 140.

CROSS-CULTURAL ISSUES IN EVANGELISM

MaryAnn Hawkins

There are, unfortunately, many Christians in the United States who believe evangelization of non-believers in other cultural contexts should utilize the same method(s) that are used in their own particular context. There may be many reasons behind this belief, but those reasons are not the focus of this writing. The focus for this writing will be on three major issues that must be addressed when considering sharing the Gospel across cultures: the language used in evangelism, the relationship between people, and the immediacy required for decision.

The word *culture* has many definitions. The definitions of "culture" that will underlay our discussion of cross-cultural evangelism are "the model for understanding reality: a system comprising all the patterns of behavior, the ideas, ways of understanding reality, and the ideal standards set by a cultural group;"[1] and "the total way of life of a group of people."[2] The way of life, the perceived reality of life, is more than how one gets food and shelter, but what is thought of as "good food" and "appropriate shelter." Culture impacts what is thought about language, about relationships, and the process for decision making.

It is also important to note that crossing cultural barriers does not necessarily mean crossing the oceans: going to a foreign country. Cultures may be generational; they may be defined by gender or socio-economics; or by "micro-cultures," i.e., specific ethnicities or

---

[1] Clinton, J. Robert. *Glossary* provided for a course in Cultural Anthropology at the School of Intercultural Studies, Fuller Theological College. 1997.

[2] Howell, Brian and Jenell Williams Paris. *Introducing Cultural Anthropology: A Christian Perspective*. Grand Rapids, MI: Baker Academic. 2011.

employment/professions; location specific,[3] or, even by education. The issues raised in this chapter can be generalized to apply to all of these.

Language

Colonialism brought English, French, and Spanish languages to most of what we now consider the *majority world*.[4] These three languages were imposed on the peoples of various nations occupied. If you wanted to be accepted by the colonizing nation you had to learn their language. The benefit to this is that both tourists and missionaries can communicate as they travel around the world. The difficult task of language learning is borne by the oppressed, the indigenous people of a country or region.

Cross-cultural evangelists must ask the question, "What does language do to the image of the God being proclaimed?" The Sabaot language translation of the New Testament was released in 1994. I had the opportunity to participate in the dedication of this new translation. A meal followed the dedicatory service and a very old woman said to me (in Swahili),[5] "Now I know that God loves me ... he speaks my language." This woman did not read any language! But the very fact that the written Word of God was in her language was enough for her to become a follower in faith: it changed her image of God.

Tammie Tregellas (SOT 1996 graduate) began her cross-cultural ministry in Kenya in 1997. I served as academic dean at KIST at the time and therefore met Tammie as she entered the country. We spent several days at a missionary guest house in Nairobi as we waited for her shipment to clear customs. During that stay a newly retired pastor from

---

[3] Location specific includes rural, suburban, urban; regional designations like "the South" or "the West Coast;" or, even locational markers like "the West Side of the city."

[4] Words previously used for this designation include: primitive, pagan, undeveloped, and developing; all of which have become denigrating to those designated by the terms. These nations and peoples make up the majority of the global population and have therefore now been identified as the *majority world*.

[5] I do not speak Sabaot, which was the language of the NT being dedicated; but it is the *heart* language of this elderly woman.

Texas was also at the guesthouse. His congregation had given him the trip as a retirement gift. He (loudly) shared each day how he planned to "minister for the Lord in Africa." One day he managed to engage a small aircraft to fly him across Kenya and Uganda to Rwanda... where he dumped Christian tracts. As he was boasting about his witness for the Lord that day, Tammie could not remain silent. She asked him what language the tracts were in: "Why, English, of course!" was his bold answer. Tammie responded with "The Rwandans speak Kirwanda,[6] Kiswahili,[7] and French. All you managed to do was provide paper for their cigarettes." Unfortunately, Tammie was correct. For all the good intentions of this pastor, his actions may well have hurt the sharing of the Gospel, the exact opposite of the outcome intended.

The language used in evangelism is, without doubt, of major concern. If the Gospel message cannot be conveyed in the language of the receiver, should evangelism be considered at all? Language, with all its forms and meanings, is a matter of culture that must be taken into consideration.

Relationship Between Persons

The next area for our consideration is the relationship between persons: the person sharing (communicating) the message being of one culture and the *receiver* of the communication being of another. For many decades cultures have been generalized as *hot* or *cold*. A *hot* culture is very expressive with both voice and gestures, generally desiring to stand close to the person they are talking with, often touching the arm or shoulder of the conversation partner. Conversely, a *cold* culture is one that speaks rather softly, without undue expression, and maintains distance from the person they are talking with. Most cultures fall somewhere between the two extremes. Another paring of cross-cultural communication terminology is *high context* and *low context*. In *high-context* cultures, "information is contained in the contexts and

---

[6] Kirwanda is the way to speak of the language of the Rwandans in Swahili.

[7] Kiswahili is the term for the Swahili language.

nonverbal cues rather than expressed explicitly in words."[8] *Low context* then is "when the information is conveyed in words rather than in nonverbal cues and contexts." Most East Asian cultures are *high context* and most American cultures, from the United States south, are *low context;* obviously there is a long continuum here as well.

Larry Sellers (missionary to Côte d'Ivoire) shared a story about the negotiation for cab transportation. The negotiation was between the cab driver and the Church of God church planter in Yamoussoukro, Côte d'Ivoire. Both men involved in the negotiation were Ivorian. Sellers witnessed yelling and dramatic gesturing such that he was fearful that it would end in a physical fight. However, the two men came to an agreement on price, shook hands, and acted like nothing happened. Larry was experiencing a *hot culture* with *low context*. Everything was communicated in words, voice, and gesture; little was left to interpretation. Conversely, it would be considered rude to speak or to make eye contact with anyone you do not know well on a bus or train in Japan. Japan is a *cold, high-context* culture. The culture is built on respect for the *other* and position in the hierarchy of society determines what an individual may say and to whom.

The Rev. Karen Helsel and her family served for many years as missionaries in Thailand (generally agreed to be a *cold, high-context* culture). They diligently learned the language, but found that in this predominately Buddhist country, it is necessary to disciple individuals **to faith** rather than discipling **after** someone comes to faith. Authentic relationships must be built over time. It is a slow process, sometimes taking years. When the word *authentic*[9] is a modifier of *relationship* it suggests that both parties are transparent, open with each other, with the ability to be one's true self in the other's presence.

---

[8] Martin, Judith N and Thomas K. Nakayama. *Experiencing Intercultural Communication: An Introduction.* Mountain View, CA: Mayfield Publishing Co. 2001.

[9] The word "authentic" is defined as "genuine" in *The Merriam-Webster Dictionary. Encarta* includes the ideas of "not fake or copied" and "valid" and *Bing* includes the synonyms of: "true, reliable, dependable, faithful, trustworthy, accurate, genuine, and realistic."

Particularly in *cold, high-context* cultures there appears to be a distrust of the words of another, unless there is authentic relationship between both communicators. This relational piece can also be seen in more *hot* or *low-context* cultures but it is often not as immediately recognized. The development of authentic relationship takes time, sharing the Gospel message cross culturally when meeting someone for the first time will generally not be received well. It may actually serve as an "inoculation" against further investigation of the Christian faith. The depth of relationship required for the receiving of the message of the Gospel is a cultural matter and must be taken into consideration in cross-cultural evangelism.

Decision Making

The macro-culture of Western Europe, generally, and the United States, particularly, includes a desire for the "instant," with "immediate" results, or to be acquired with ease. We have instant coffee and puddings and we have "drive-through" eateries, even drive-in churches. We want everything "now." Beginning about the midway of the 1900s, there was also the idea that people, as individuals, should be confronted by the Gospel and make, as an individual, an immediate decision to follow Christ. The approach for cross-cultural evangelism was perceived as being the same. A group of evangelists[10] might go into a neighborhood or district and confront everyone they meet with the Gospel: being invited (at best) or coerced (at worst) to make an immediate decision to become a follower of Christ(ianity). This methodology did work in many places, but in others, Christ(ianity) was rejected simply because of the required immediate decision.

There are many cultures that place significant value on community. These hold that the community (tribe, clan, village, extended family) should discuss any/every issue and make the appropriate decision for the community: this would be considered as decision by consensus.

---

[10] Trained or untrained, often self-proclaimed evangelists or missionaries. Persons whose hearts were often in the right place but without the cultural understanding of a specific place.

In 1998 there was a group of students and faculty[11] who went to an unreached area of Mt. Elgon in Kenya. They held outdoor services each evening and visited people throughout the village during the day. They did not share the Gospel with intent for immediate decision as they visited during the day; they simply invited people to the outdoor evening services. The villagers were invited at the close of each service to talk to the students if they wanted to know more about Christ. As the two week evangelism/outreach progressed, no one responded. The students did begin to see small groups of men[12] (and some women) gathering each day for conversation. On the next to the last evening a female Tanzanian student named Esther was assigned to preach. At the close she again invited people who were interested in knowing more to talk to the students who had come. For several minutes no one moved. Then, an old man stood and moved forward to talk to Esther. Almost immediately people stood and gathered around the various students asking questions about entering into a relationship with the Creator God through Jesus Christ as Savior. The village and its surrounding area responded to the call of the Gospel as a group: a consensus had been reached.

The speed at which a decision is demanded and whether the decision is required individually or in community is a matter of culture and must therefore be taken into consideration in cross-cultural evangelism.

Conclusion

As a student of the Christian Scriptures, I believe that the call of God to make disciples of ALL peoples is given and received as a mandate. The Scriptures are replete with the call to be witnesses, to be a light, to care for the strangers because of God's desire for reconciliation with humankind: this is the *missio Dei*. There are, however, a multitude of barriers that must be negotiated to effectively witness cross culturally. Three of those barriers have been discussed in this chapter. Dr. Charles

---

[11] Students and faculty were from the Kima International School of Theology: individuals originating from Kenya, Tanzania, Uganda, Rwanda, and the United States.

[12] This area was/is highly patriarchal.

Van Engen has stated that "the more barriers that need to be crossed, the more energy that is required by the missionary (cross-cultural communicator).[13] Cross-cultural evangelism finds no short cut for sharing the Gospel. It calls for people who are willing to do the hard work of language learning, who are willing to take the time to establish authentic relationships, and who are willing to wait on the readiness of decision making. The difficulty represented should not be allowed to thwart the sharing of the Gospel cross culturally. A life in relationship with God, reconciled to God by the sacrificial life of Jesus the Christ is the life that God desires for all of humankind. Learning how best to share the life-giving nature of the Gospel of the Kingdom of God should be approached with excitement, even joy, as it is the highest calling to be a witness to the nations.

---

[13] Class notes: Charles Van Engen, School of Intercultural Studies, Fuller Theological Seminary, 1998.

EVANGELISM IN THE LARGE CHURCH

Marty Grubbs

The calendar year 2014 finds me in my 33rd year as a resident of Oklahoma City and a staff member of what is now known as Crossings Community Church. Throughout my journey in ministry, David Sebastian has been ever present in numerous ways.

He pastored a larger church that gave me an example to follow and ideas to try. He brought one of the great worship leaders of the Church of God, George Skramstad, to the forefront as a member of his staff in Arizona who would later spend 20 years on my staff. David became the senior pastor of my home church, The Salem Church of God in Dayton, Ohio. He came from the same town where my mother was born, (Middletown, Ohio) where my grandparents lived all of their married lives, and my mom, Dolly, Uncle Courtney Duff, Aunt Joan Martin and their families still reside. His name was frequently mentioned as one highly respected.

There was great celebration when David became the dean of our seminary. He brought such unique gifts and experiences to the task. Then, as a senior pastor, it was my privilege to be invited to a gathering launched by David for other Church of God pastors whose congregations had grown beyond 500 in attendance. And still today, he initiates that gathering, providing great inspiration and fellowship. He continues to encourage those who have the difficult task of leading congregations of all sizes, small and large alike. I write as one who has been fortunate to call him friend. I write as one who was influenced by David's efforts in getting me acquainted with some of the largest congregations in America.

Occasionally, I read that the church I pastor is doomed. Its demise is certain. Not because the world is turning from God, not because people are not interested in Christianity, but simply because my church is large. The small neighborhood congregation I agreed to lead in October 1985 is now, by definition, a mega-church. To be truthful, I don't like that word. One research group says the younger generation is repulsed just driving by our building, and another research group says that the large church will only get larger and, in fact, it says more small congregations will merge with larger ones. So confusing. When the coffee cup is empty, and my scheduled time for reading is over, I find myself walking into a church, yes, a large church, yes, a mega-church. Ugh! However, what I see is a very vibrant ministry booming with a young generation I was told would not be interested. So I just keep my focus and get to work. I know what is working in Oklahoma City so I just stay with it.

As I indicated earlier, I was asked to be the senior pastor of the church where I had served initially in my ministry as associate pastor. The church had a marvelous start with one of our finest, Dr. Dwight Dye, and had been led by three other pastors I grew to deeply respect and value. I came along in the congregation's 22nd year of ministry and at year 26 was asked to be their senior pastor. These fabulous people were eager to impact the community. They wanted to shine the light of Christ brightly in our community. But for reasons few of us fully understood, the church had not experienced any significant growth in many years. The original group of 55 people had grown to a church of 150 people, landed in a beautiful north side neighborhood of Oklahoma City, and had a nice building complete with a large kitchen and gymnasium, ample youth space, Sunday school space, and a very elegant but small 200 seat sanctuary.

It was my great fortune to grow up in the home of one of the greatest pastors I will ever know. I remember as a very young boy, of probably 5 years of age, walking through the new church being built in Kingsport, Tenn., to house the growing congregation led by my father, David Grubbs. I remember crawling through the new construction of a larger 1,000 seat sanctuary in Dayton, Ohio, yet again making room for a growing congregation. And I remember walking the 65 acre campus and seeing the footprint of a new 100,000 square foot building to house that same rapidly growing church. When I moved to Oklahoma City in 1981, it was the smallest congregation I had ever been a part of. And when it wasn't growing, something seemed odd. I soon realized that I had never been a part of a church that was not growing. As I reflected on that reality, I was reminded of the various ingredients that seemed to be ever present in the growing congregations of my formative years. The word that came to mind was "evangelism."

We don't hear much of that word these days. But I believe evangelism is still very much at the core purpose of the church. In my youth, evangelism was a program. Today it is a lifestyle. Then, it was something you did. Today it is who you are. Let me explain.

Forty years ago I was trained to use the simple tool called "The Four Spiritual Laws." This was the brainchild of Dr. Bill Bright, founder of Campus Crusade. The four laws were easy to use, easy to carry, and easy to leave on the table when you left the restaurant. I've heard far too many angry accusations toward Christians from restaurant staff because someone left a four-laws tract in place of a tip. And someone thought that was evangelism?! Please understand that I have high respect and admiration for both the person and ministry of Dr. Bill Bright. It is not a negative reflection on him that his idea was misused by some Christians. I think Christians at that time assumed people needed information. And the information they needed, we said, was to inform them of the chance they could go to hell if they did not receive this "gift" we were giving them. I have long felt that, in the routine attempts by Christians to "evangelize" with this information, we drove far more people away from Christ than to him.

My next dose of evangelism training came from a program called "Evangelism Explosion." While the word "explosion" today may not serve us well, EE, as we called it, was a top-notch training program that drove home the point of sharing your personal experience with Christ. I was a part of EE in my home church in Dayton and later would bring it to my church in Oklahoma City. When I first started in EE, we went out to the homes of those who had visited the church the previous Sunday. We did not call ahead or schedule an appointment. If, by chance, none of our visitor cards yielded an open door, we had been trained to start cold calling. Go to the mall, stand outside the grocery store, approach people on the sidewalk. I will admit that the cold calling piece of this program was my least favorite. By the time I was using "Evangelism

Explosion" in my church in Oklahoma City, an unannounced visit to a door was a deal killer. So we used various approaches to secure an appointment prior to heading to someone's home. The content was still the same. It was a simple outline consisting of several elements. We would start with a friendly visit about any matter of subjects in an attempt to find common ground. Then we moved to the personal testimony phase. Finally, we closed by presenting the gospel and asking if they were ready to make a commitment. And many were ready. It was effective. But as they say, "the times, they were a-changing."

As the seeker movement began to take center stage in American Christianity, we moved from a confrontational style of evangelism to a relational approach. Rather than gathering at the church for training and then heading out for visits, the sermons being preached were "how-to" sermons, many of them on building a bridge to unsaved friends and acquaintances. And it worked. The seeker-sensitive movement taught us to show genuine concern for those around us in hopes of earning the right to share our conversion story. It was a new day for that old word evangelism.

The primary focus of seeker-sensitive congregations was the non-believer, the outsider, those dealing with the pain that life throws at us. The key evangelism approach of the large church became an honest and transparent pulpit where no subject was off limits. The common sermon themes were aimed specifically at the core issues of the day. In fact, the sermon series that lit the spark of growth in my church in 1988 was a 12-week series based on the 12 steps of Alcoholics Anonymous. I had never attended an AA meeting, but I had a friend who thought I might find the steps to be very helpful in providing smaller, more manageable steps to a better life. As I prepared the message topics, my team was busy finding ways to communicate this new series to the community. We did some advertising in the local newspaper. However, more importantly, we mailed a postcard about the series to every home within two square miles of the church. One of our leaders asked me if I was prepared for the "type of people" who might come through the door while speaking on this topic. In his mind, he was thinking of the stereotypical guy that stumbles in either drunk or having a bad hangover. But a great surprise was in store for us.

The series started and the people showed up. Attendance nearly doubled. But it wasn't the hung over or the drunk who came. The people came from all walks of life, the finest of homes, and the highest of positions in the community. They were either dealing with an issue in their life, or they had a family member who was. What started out as a sermon series drove us to start a very different type of Sunday school class, small groups or recovery groups during the week, and pay for Christian counseling if needed. The outgrowth of this "evangelistic" effort is still very evident today in the ministries of a large counseling center in the church, a Monday night "Care Series" which includes divorce recovery, 12 Step meetings, and various support groups rallying around a variety of heartbreaking issues. The sermon series of 1988 served not only to reach people never before seen in any church, it also created a mindset and attitude within the church that it was no longer "about us." Thankfully and gratefully, the change continues. Crossings has embraced the challenge of evangelism in ways I could have never imagined or predicted. I see the current landscape dealing with several challenges.

First of all, this current young generation wants to know exactly what we think and believe, and they want to know why we believe it. They can handle the hard truth. They want to know the facts and why I think those facts are important. They want to know why I am willing to live my life according to those principles.

Second, they want relationships to be real and genuine. They will not allow themselves to become a project for someone who has an agenda. They want to be heard and valued.

Third, they respond to transparency. Come across as one who has it all together or has all the answers, and they will walk away. They want to know if you are one who struggles with things just like they do.

Fourth, they want to know if you really care. A pastor of a church of any size must aggressively seek to understand the cultural context in which they have been called to minister. The pace of change in our culture is staggering. Dr. Sebastian in his new book *Recovering Our Nerve* makes a profound and relevant statement: "With change, there is usually a degree of discomfort, for change is often perceived as loss and loss creates grief. This is why churches must learn to navigate cultural change successfully or face the possibility of irrelevance or demise."[1] I've always been challenged by 1 Chronicles 12:32, "from Issachar, men who understood the times and knew what Israel should do" (NIV). I believe the key to effective evangelism is to understand the day in which we live, seek to understand the people around you, and live out a real and genuine Christ-centered life.

Crossings leased an old Wal-Mart 10 years ago and opened a fulltime free medical clinic and developed a community center. To date, our clinic has served nearly 50,000 people from all walks of life. The community center has become a place for afterschool programs, such as tutoring and sports activity. This ministry brought evangelistic opportunities in ways I could not have predicted. The obvious and predicted evangelism opportunity came with those we served in this ministry. We assumed this type of care, on their turf, would open the door to the gospel, and it has. People saw a church doing something away from the large campus, meeting significant needs on a daily basis. Many younger folks have volunteered because they are on a mission to fix the world's problems. They are rebelling from the materialism of their Baby Boomer parents and grandparents. They are very sensitive to the poor and marginalized. As volunteers, they encountered a group of very committed followers of Christ.

Our commitment to evangelism takes us to eight inner-city schools where we minister on a weekly basis. We buy all school supplies for every teacher every year. We provide Christmas gifts to every student in all eight schools. The people of Crossings play "Santa" every year and fulfill the wishes of nearly 2,000 kids. We do not insist on handing out Bibles in the classroom or starting Bible studies in the schools. We simply serve and love because we have been served and loved by Jesus.

This is evangelism in the larger church setting. This is evangelism in Oklahoma City. This is evangelism at Crossings Community Church. Evangelism today for the larger congregation is often a satellite location in another part of the city or even in another town. Evangelism

---

[1] David L. Sebastian, *Recovering Our Nerve: A Primer for Evangelism in Everyday Life* (Anderson: Warner Press, 2013), 37.

---

is mobilizing large groups of people to impact their neighborhood. Evangelism is offering classes on Wednesday nights of high interest to the community at large. We find success in evangelism as we patiently answer questions of the non-believer, where we do not demand an immediate decision at the end of a worship service, where we make it clear that we are willing to walk with them regardless of any possible decision. We find success when we first ask the question, "What do you need?"

I want to add as I conclude that I have a very deep love for the smaller church. My colleagues in smaller congregations work much harder than I do. We at Crossings have a very strong desire to encourage and support the local church pastor in the context of a smaller setting. In other words, evangelism in the larger church must be not only for that congregation but also for any church that could benefit from the partnership with us.

The approach to evangelism in our large church is not that different from what we started doing as a small congregation. To be sure, we did not have money then to open clinics and community centers, buy supplies for eight schools, or start satellite sites around the city. But we did have a strong desire to reach people, a strong desire truly to help people get through whatever they were going through, and a strong desire to be a visible demonstration of the love of Christ to everyone we encounter. In 1988, we did this one person at a time, one relationship at a time. And those same principles are guiding us today.

LEADERSHIP

EFFECTIVE LEADERSHIP

John H. Aukerman

Robert H. Reardon, president of Anderson College (1958-1983), illustrated several core leadership principles with what we students knew as the "Uncle Barney Story,"[1] which he read every year in the Christmas Chapel. I sat in those chapels, at age 18, 19, and 20, but never really listened to the story. As a result, its meaning and depth were lost on me. But in recent years I found it on the internet and now I read it to my seminary students, during the first class of the semester and again during our final meeting. Why? Because it vividly demonstrates that all effective leaders, like Uncle Barney, do two important things: (1) they define tasks for groups, and (2) they practice human relations skills. And they do it in a way that matches the needs of the group.

Leadership Theory

There is a popular belief that people either *have* or *don't have* leadership ability. However, a massive amount of research in the second half of the 20th century failed to uncover any underlying personality trait in leaders. The evidence seems to suggest that leadership is a skill that can be learned: people can learn how to define tasks for groups, and they can learn effective human relations skills.

A.W. Halpin and B.J. Winer, of The Ohio State University, identified and described the two dimensions of effective leadership: consideration and initiating structure.[2] *Consideration* reflects the extent

---

[1] Written by Leah Newstadt, "Let's Go Neighboring," *Guideposts,* 1954. Available at http://homeandholidays.com/lets-go-neighboring/.

[2] http://changingminds.org/disciplines/leadership/actions/ohio_state.htm.

to which the leader shows behavior that is indicative of friendship, mutual trust, respect, and warmth in relationships with group members. Genuine consideration by the leader reflects an awareness of the needs of each member of the group. Leaders high in this characteristic encourage group members to communicate with them and to share their feelings. *Initiating structure* is the degree to which a leader defines and structures his or her role and the roles of the subordinates toward achieving the goals of the group.

Social science researchers have discovered combinations of *leader characteristics and behaviors,* and *group member characteristics* that interact to produce effective group life and accomplishment. Effective and useful results have emerged.

Leader Characteristics and Behaviors

Leader characteristics and behaviors vary along two dimensions, closely related to consideration and initiating structure: relationship behavior and task behavior, and most leader behaviors can be classified as either *relationship actions* or *task actions.* Paul Hersey and Kenneth Blanchard define relationship behavior as the extent to which a leader engages in two-way communication by providing emotional support and facilitating behaviors. They define task behavior as the extent to which a leader engages in one-way communication by explaining what a person is to do, as well as when, where, and how to do it.[3]

Any leader of any group can estimate her tendency toward relationship behavior or task behavior by simply counting the number one-way communications and two-way communications she sends. If she desires a less-biased estimate, she can ask members of her group to count her one-way communications and two-way communications over a period of time. The raw numbers will give a rough estimate of her tendency toward task behavior or relationship behavior.

For purposes of understanding a leader's task vs. relationship behavior, Hersey and Blanchard found it useful to view all leader

---

[3] Paul Hersey and Kenneth Blanchard, *Management of Organizational Behavior: Utilizing Human Resources* (Englewood Cliffs, NJ: Prentice Hall, 1996).

behavior as either high or low. There is no continuum, no gradation; a leader is either high task or low task; high relationship or low relationship. A particular leader may find himself in one of four conditions:

1. high task and low relationship
2. high task and high relationship
3. low task and high relationship
4. low task and low relationship

Each one of these four kinds of leaders may be effective or ineffective, depending on the situation. Which particular combination of leader behaviors is most appropriate depends on the characteristics of the group members.

Group Member Characteristics

The key concept in understanding the group member characteristics is maturity. We are not interested in physical, mental, or emotional maturity; the maturity at issue here is the group members'

1. capacity to set high but attainable goals (achievement motivation),

2. willingness and ability to take responsibility, and

3. education and/or experience of group members.

Maturity is always determined in relation to a specific task to be performed; on one task a group can have high maturity, while on another task it will have low maturity. If a group meets all three conditions, it has high maturity. If it meets none of the conditions, it has low maturity. And if it meets one or two of the conditions, it has moderately low or moderately high maturity, respectively.

Here is an example of what this looks like in real life and ministry. When I served as pastor, our congregation had a Sunday school growth campaign (this was back in the days when Sunday schools were still growing!). We asked each class to set a growth goal for the six weeks of the campaign. All but one class set reasonable growth goals. This one class, of about 15 adults, said that they would double in size over six weeks. When put to the three-fold test of maturity, this class measured low:

1. It set a high but unattainable goal (which indicates low achievement motivation).

2. It was not willing or able to take responsibility (members took no action to reach their goal).

3. It had no education and/or experience in growth.

Not meeting even one of the three conditions, this group was "low maturity." At the time this happened, I had not learned about Hersey and Blanchard's situational leadership model, so I was of no help to this class. Now, however, I recognize such a goal as a telltale sign that the group needed a particular kind of leader.

Leader-Member Combinations for Effective Leadership

The essence of Hersey and Blanchard's theory is that when a group has low maturity in terms of a specific task, the leader should engage in high task/low relationship behaviors. When the group is moderately immature, the leader should move to high task/high relationship behaviors, and then to low task/high relationship behaviors as the group reaches moderate maturity. When the group is highly mature in terms of accomplishing a specific task, then low task/low relationship behaviors are needed. Sometimes a picture helps:

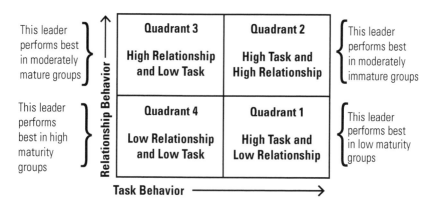

That adult Sunday school class, because it was a low maturity group, needed a Quadrant 1 leader, high task and low relationship. This would be a leader who engaged mostly in one-way communication, a leader who would *tell* the class what to do, how to do it, when to do it, etc. A results-oriented leader was needed, because the group was low maturity.

However, if the class had passed one of the three tests of maturity (indicating moderate immaturity), it would have needed a leader from Quadrant 2, high task and high relationship. This leader would engage in lots of one-way *and* two-way communication, functioning more as a coach to the class as it tried to grow.

Further, had the class passed two of the three tests of maturity (moderately mature), it would have needed a Quadrant 3 leader: a *participant* who practiced mostly two-way communication. And finally, if the class passed all three tests of maturity (highly mature), it would have needed a Quadrant 4 leader, a *delegator,* who would have minimized communication (low task and low behavior).

Here is another way to picture this. As a group increases in maturity (capacity to set high but attainable goals, willingness and ability to take responsibility, and education and/or experience of group members), its leader needs to move through the four quadrants in this order:

	Quadrant 3	Quadrant 2
Relationship Behavior	High Relationship and Low Task	High Task and High Relationship
	Quadrant 4	Quadrant 1
	High Maturity and Low Task	Low Maturity Low Relationship

Task Behavior ⟶

The leader would move from telling to coaching to participating to delegating. Therefore effective leaders must be flexible: when they discern that the group is maturing, they must modify their leadership style. This is the difficult part of leadership — many leaders have one set of preferred skills and the thought of changing to a different skill set never occurs to them. And even if it does occur, many leaders lack the self awareness, self confidence, and personal discipline to change their style. The perceptive reader will take this to heart and will make it a matter of personal resolve to change their leadership style when the group matures and needs a different kind of leader. I close with a story that illustrates effective leadership, a man who provided a different kind of leadership when the situation called for it, like Uncle Barney did.

The Man Who Remembered[4]
By Lorin F. Wheelwright

Sometimes when we grow old we forget. But this is a story of a man who remembered.

He was a giant of a man and in his Alpine village everyone called him Magnus — meaning big. Although his muscles were tough from climbing many times, his heart was tender for his little boy, Angelo.

When spring finally came, Magnus took little Angelo by the hand and said, "Son, you are old enough to climb the mountain; come with me." Off they went, Magnus the giant and little Angelo running at his heels. The neighbors smiled as they saw the two of them head for the mountain. At the edge of town, old Solomon, cried out from his shop, "Be careful, Magnus; don't you lose that little angel in the mountains." With a swing of his arms, Magnus answered by lifting the boy above his head, and off he strode, like a proud elephant with his small driver astride his mighty shoulders.

---

[4] Lorin F. Wheelwright, "The Man Who Remembered," *The Instructor,* 1969, 234-235, accessed March 20, 2014, https://archive.org/stream/instructor1047dese#page/n7/mode/2up/search/wheelwright.

After climbing for a long time, with Angelo sometimes running, sometimes riding, Magnus saw the high cliff, and through the underbrush he spotted a little glen by a stream. He said to Angelo, "Let's rest here by this pool and eat our lunch." He lifted his little boy to the ground and Angelo ran to the stream and dipped his face into the fresh, clear water. They ate their cheese and bread, and as Magnus stretched out for a little rest, he sank into the soft grass and murmured, "Angelo, stay close by; we'll soon be going home."

Angelo did not hear, or pretended not to, because he wanted to put his face in that water again — it felt so cool and tasted so good. As he leaned over, a gentle breeze carried the fragrance of mountain violets to his nostrils, and he turned to see where they grew — and there they were in little clusters by the stream. His legs flew as up the hillside he climbed to pick the purple flowers.

As he leaned over one cluster, he saw a large rock; and from under it the water was bubbling up. To see more clearly he pushed aside some bushes beside the rock, and there to his amazement was a hole. "Is this where the mountain hides its water?" he asked himself. "I shall find out." And in through the hole he crawled.

It was dark inside; only a faint glow from a few rays of the sun lit the dim cavern. As he crept forward, his foot dislodged a rock and he heard it rumble down below and the sound echoed on and on, never seeming to end. He called out, "Haloo!" and heard his voice again and again — and it sounded big and deep, like that of his father. Never had he heard anything like this, so he sat down and began to talk to the mountain.

Down by the pool, Magnus awakened with a start. He jumped to his feet and called, "Angelo! Angelo! Where are you?" but there was no answer. Frantically he climbed to the top of the cliff, but he could see nothing of his little Angelo. Inside his heaving shoulders he felt the sharp pain of fear — it drove him back down the rocks to the pool, and there in despair he fell to his knees and sobbed out his prayer to God. "Help me find my little Angelo," he cried. As he opened his eyes he looked into the water at his own troubled face. There he saw a strange sight — something long forgotten — looking back from the mirrored pool was not the face of Magnus, the giant, but the face of Magnus, the boy. He knelt closer to see if it were some strange formation of rocks that made him see this long-forgotten image. As he leaned over the bank, he caught the fragrance of mountain violets. On his knees he followed their scent and remembered a childhood adventure in the mountains.

Faster he scrambled up the side of the stream until he came to the rock, and there it was — the bubbling spring, and beside it, hidden behind the bushes, the hole where once he had entered the mountain and heard it speak. He stood up and pulled away the bushes, but he could not crawl in, the opening was so small and he was so big. He shook with terror as he imagined his Angelo in the cavern alone and lost. Back to his knees he fell and with a prayer on his lips he wiggled and squirmed his way through the small tunnel.

Once inside he lay panting on the damp earth and then, faintly above the pounding of his own heart, he heard a distant sound, echoing over and over, "Haloo! – Haloo! – Haloo!" He answered, "Angelo! – Angelo! – Angelo!"

In the dim light he could not see his little boy, but he could hear little feet running toward him; and in a moment he reached out into the darkness and clasped his son to his heart. Then Angelo spoke, "Daddy, Daddy, how did you find me?"

And Magnus, with tears running down his cheeks, sobbed, half answering and half praying a thanksgiving. "Son," he said, "I found you by becoming a child again."

And in that village, they still talk about Magnus, the giant, who remembered to become as a little child so he could enter the mighty mountain and find his lost son.

LEADERSHIP:
THE CHALLENGE AND GIFTEDNESS
OF YOUNG PASTORS

Matthew Anderson

And don't let anyone put you down because you're young. Teach believers with your life: by word, by demeanor, by love, by faith, by integrity. Stay at your post reading Scripture, giving counsel, teaching. And that special gift of ministry you were given when the leaders of the church laid hands on you and prayed keep that dusted off and in use (1 Timothy 4:12-13, MSG).

A s a young youth pastor, I loved this passage of scripture. It gave me the courage to be bold, and I used it to inspire students to be bold. For at least the past 30 years, this passage of scripture has provided a mantra for youth pastors and youth alike. Paul, writing to his young apprentice, was encouraging Timothy to be bold with the message of Christ, the good news with which he had been entrusted. He was charging this young pastor to live a life marked by integrity. Paul was reminding Timothy of that purpose to which he had been called by God. This short passage of scripture gives us a glimpse of both the challenges young leaders face and the giftedness young leaders bring into the church today.

Relationship

Behind this passage of scripture was a relationship. The apostle Paul was a mentor to Timothy. According to Acts chapter 16, Paul met Timothy in Lystra. Timothy was a disciple who had a good reputation among the believers in this region. Paul invited Timothy to join his journey, visiting the churches that he had established and continuing to spread the good news of Jesus. Over the course of time, Paul invested in young Timothy, and, after parting ways, wrote him two letters of encouragement and instruction. It could be argued that without Paul as a mentor, Timothy might not have ever pursued his calling as a leader in the early church.

Young pastors in the church desperately need mentors and coaches who will invest in, encourage, and challenge them. Young leaders bring much to the table: energy, connectivity, cultural awareness, etc. Yet their perspective and life experience is limited. Mentors and coaches bring a perspective and wisdom that cannot be learned in a classroom or read in a book. Personal relationship is interactive and exploratory. It has the potential to guide the young leader to a place s/he could not have traveled alone. Timothy needed Paul. And young pastors today need intentional, mentoring relationships with those who have a wider perspective and experience.

Credibility
Teach believers with your life.

One of the greatest challenges of leadership is influence. Many of us assume that once we are given a position or title, we will assume a level of influence, we will be given a voice with a people. But a title, a position of leadership, will never create or produce influence. Credibility is the only currency of leadership. Credibility is earned over time, with every act of integrity and care and love. Steve Saccone writes, "A character-driven leader is a leader who becomes a person with something to say. Their life compels others to listen."[1] And this is why Paul encourages Timothy toward a life that reflects something worth following.

Credibility, for the young pastor, flows out of deeply formed Christ-centered character. N. T. Wright defines this formation: "Here is the real challenge: not just to add one or two more commandments, to set the moral bar a little higher, but to become a different sort of person altogether. Jesus is challenging the young man to a transformation of

---

[1] Steve Saccone, *Protégé: Developing Your Next Generation of Church Leaders* (Downers Grove, IL: IVP Books., 2012), chapter 1, Kindle Edition.

character."[2] He goes on, suggesting that "character is a slowly forming thing. You can no more force character on someone than you can force a tree to produce fruit when it isn't ready to do so. The person has to choose, again and again, to develop the moral muscles and skills which will shape and form the fully flourishing character" (ch. 1). The challenge for young leaders is to allow character transformation to happen according to God's Spirit. It cannot be created or forced. And this slowly forming character, over time, leads to credibility with others. And again, credibility is the only true currency of leadership.

Pastor
Stay at your post.

Quite a few years ago, our church staff spent some time working through personality and strength testing. We wanted to learn more about each other — our strengths and personality traits. Not only did it achieve that purpose, but it also helped us learn how we could work well together, utilizing each team member's strengths. For years, personality, strength and psychological testing have been popular in business for this very reason. But out of this exercise, we discovered a challenge to leadership on the team. Once strengths were discovered, the tendency for some team members, especially the younger staff, was to work only in their areas of giftedness and set aside those tasks that did not match their strengths. For example, one pastor discovered that he had strengths in strategy, administration, and visioning. He decided he would set aside hospital visitation and spiritual direction as they were outside of his primary giftedness. The challenge for young pastors here is to remain faithful to the pastoral tasks that are essential in our calling, no matter the core strengths and competencies we may have.

The pastoral vocation encompasses functions that all pastors must fulfill. Eugene Peterson writes, "Three pastoral acts are so basic, so critical, that they determine the shape of everything else. The acts

---

[2] N.T. Wright, *After You Believe: Why Christian Character Matters* (New York, NY: Harper-Collins, 2010), chapter 1, Kindle Edition.

are praying, reading Scripture, and giving spiritual direction."[3] This is the foundation of the pastoral vocation and is shared by all those called to lead within the context of the local church. In our world of diversification and specialization in ministry, a challenge young pastors face is the temptation to set aside the pastoral acts that are essential to the church community. Paul instructs Timothy to "Stay at your post reading scripture, giving counsel, teaching," for these are the tasks to which all pastors are called to engage.

Voice
And that special gift of ministry you were given...

Each of us is given a voice. That voice is unique to each pastor. Sitting at a roundtable with Leith Anderson, we heard him talk of his early days of ministry. He told us that he could not get any traction with his church or community in Colorado. Everything was difficult. When he felt as though things were starting to click, something would derail the momentum. He made the difficult decision to step away from this church and pastor in the Minneapolis area. It was not long before Leith felt something he had never experienced before. The community resonated with his voice, and momentum moved this church community to influence and impact the larger community. As he talked of this experience, he looked at a few of the young leaders who were sitting around the table and said, "Don't ever underestimate when God gives you the voice to speak to a community."

All of us can get caught up in the success-driven models of our American culture. Even with pure hearts, we can easily slip off track and find ourselves desiring more and bigger and better. God can use our voice and our gifts in many different locations and in many different expressions of the local church. But there are times when he calls us to a specific location for a specific purpose. Paul challenged young Timothy to "keep that [special gift of ministry] dusted off and in use." Young

---

[3] Eugene Peterson. *Working the Angles: The Shape of Pastoral Integrity* (Grand Rapids, MI: Wm. B. Eerdmans Publishing Co., 1987), 3. Kindle Edition.

pastors and leaders must fight the temptation to look beyond current posts and remain faithfully engaged in that work to which he has called us.

When I was young in my formation and ministry, Andy Stanley and Rob Bell were unique voices in the larger church community. I listened to and watched them. They spoke to my soul and stretched my perspectives. Soon, I found myself emulating them in my preaching and leadership. I tried to think and speak like them. One Sunday, a trusted friend said to me, "Matt, God didn't call Andy to lead our church, he called you. We don't need you to be Andy, we need you to be you." I was embarrassed and a little defensive. But God's Spirit worked in me through that confrontation. He reminded me that I had been given a voice, and that my voice was exactly what was needed for the task which I had been given. In our culture of information accessibility, we all must fight the temptation simply to copy the voice of others. This is not to say that we, as pastors and leaders, cannot utilize the deep well of material provided by technology, but we must develop the voice God has given us, unique to each of us. God calls us. He gifts us. He develops us. We must give him the space and time and do this work in us rather than attempt to copy the work he has done in another.

A Final Word

Three thousand young leaders from across denominations had gathered to sharpen their leadership and find rest for their souls. Catalyst West (2011) had been programmed for this very purpose. Space was created to give the Holy Spirit room to renew the souls of these leaders, many of whom were on the edge of burnout and depression. Time was spent encouraging and building up these young leaders. And mature, seasoned leaders spoke wisdom and challenge to this next generation of pastoral leadership in the church. Eugene Peterson was one of those who challenged these young leaders. He spent time talking about his own life, his calling into the pastoral vocation, and the walking out of that leadership in the church. He spoke of events in his life that were formational, challenging those in attendance to consider how they, too, were being formed by God. Finally, he gave these young leaders a caution and a charge as they returned to their leadership posts in and around local churches: "The caution would be that we don't allow the culture to define our position, our vocation." And herein lies the most daunting challenge for young leaders in the church. In a culture of leadership development, success orientation, and self-promotion, young leaders must rest in their vocation as a calling of God not to be defined by the culture in which they live. Leaders in God's Kingdom are called to be followers first, to leave results in the hands of the Holy Spirit and to remain humble, dying to one's self.

The church should be optimistic about her future. Young pastors are being called and equipped to lead the local church in joining God's mission of redeeming and restoring a broken world. These young leaders bring energy and excitement, connectivity and creativity. As they are mentored and coached in this pastoral vocation and as God transforms their character and develops their voice by the work of the Holy Spirit, the church will continue to move the Kingdom of God forward in the world today. As leaders in the church, we have been handed the keys of that kingdom. May we be faithful in throwing open the doors and ushering in those who are turning back to God by the work of Jesus Christ.

WHEN IT'S TIME TO LEAVE

Diana L. Swoope

Nothing will last forever. Endings are not only recurrent but are requisite. As the prophet of Ecclesiastes affirms, "To everything there is a season; a time for every purpose under heaven: A time to be born and a time to die; a time to plant, and a time to pluck what is planted" (Ecclesiastes 3:1-2, NKJV). The prophet implies that there is a time to arrive and there is a time to depart; a time to lead and a time to leave. Everything has a life cycle in which beginnings are released and in which endings are required. Throughout his celebrated journey as a leader, David Sebastian has been on both the beginning and ending side of the leadership cycle; he has been both the predecessor and the successor.

Passing the baton is said to be the absolute most important transaction to occur in a relay race. If the baton transfer is bobbled or mishandled in any way, the team stands to lose ground and perhaps lose the race altogether. A dropped baton, though not necessarily resulting in disqualification, will certainly shatter the hopes of winning at any level. Teams will practice this handoff maneuver repeatedly in order to gain fluidity of motion, proper hand placement and even to establish the speed of approach in the handoff zone — all in an effort to ensure the completion of a smooth transfer. The runners are fully aware that a smooth handoff is more important than speed, for the baton is the symbol of the race itself.

Leadership transitions can be compared to the passing of a baton in a relay race. The baton represents the transfer of power and authority, it is the past meeting the future; it is in effect the symbol of the forward progression of the organization. How the ending of a runner's lap is negotiated is absolutely crucial for the sustaining of the race. The current runner has greater control of the baton passing maneuver and as such must act with extreme confidence at this juncture and give leadership to the process. In like manner, the actions of the outgoing leader can serve to make or break the fluidity of the transition within an organization. One author contends that "Smooth, effective leadership transitions happen when thoughtful planning occurs and when the outgoing chief executive collaborates effectively with board leadership and the organization's senior leadership team in a transparent and inclusive way."[1] This type of communication may be very difficult for the transitioning leader no matter how long the person has been in leadership. It may be particularly difficult if she or he is the founder or has led the organization for a lengthy period of time.

There are a plethora of emotions that may directly impact the initiation of this conversation. Sometimes it is difficult for the leader to know when to exit. Other leaders may burn out or linger long after their effectiveness has diminished. Some may know it is time to depart but are not in a financial position to leave. Sometimes the leader's self definition is threatened by the very idea of letting go because she or he has been in the role for so long. A transitioning seminary president was surprised at the degree to which he had lost his personal identity during his lengthy tenure at the institution. While it is usually unintentional, he stated that serving in one place for many years "did more than allow you to define an institution. The institution began to define you."[2]

Letting go can be difficult and the leader would do well to gain the help of a trusted counselor to help navigate the many inevitable emotions. Still, it is wise to recognize that all leaders come to go. The sober reality is that every leader will leave the organization whether through retirement, resignation, moving to another job or even sadly through some catastrophic circumstance such as a debilitating illness or death. She or he would do well to prepare personally for this inevitability. Equally, the leader of integrity will take responsibility

---

[1] P. R. Wendell, *When Leaders Leave: A New Perspective on Leadership Change* (Philadelphia: MarketShift, Inc., 2013), 51.

[2] Heather Grennan Gary, "A Graceful Exit," *In Trust,* New Year 2012, accessed March 21, 2014, http://www.intrust.org/portals/39/docs/SpotlightArticle.pdf.

to prepare the organization for a successful change in leadership. For, like the passing of the baton in the relay race, the successful handoff of leadership can help to preserve the organization and the trust of its stakeholders, and allow it to be in a position to grow and adapt to meet new challenges with imagination and zeal.

One author used four symbolic roles to depict the different ways in which a leader departs and the potential impact it has upon the organization using the description of "monarchs, generals, ambassadors and governors."

- **Monarchs** do not exit until they are forced out by ill health (or death) or by some form of palace revolution, such as the resignation of top managers or an action of the board.

- **Generals** also depart under force. They leave reluctantly while plotting their return to rescue the organization from the real or imagined inadequacy of their successor.

- **Ambassadors** leave gracefully. They frequently serve as mentors after they retire. They tend to remain on the board of directors. They provide continuity and counsel for their successor and the organization.

- **Governors** rule for a limited term, then shift to another vocational outlet after their exit. They tend to maintain little or no continuing contact with the organization.[3]

This writer submits that David Sebastian would best be depicted as an ambassador, leaving his positions gracefully and thoughtfully, making an easier path in which his successors can follow and a stronger platform upon which the organization can stand. While a smooth transition does not tacitly guarantee future success for the organization (some organizations have actually become weakened despite a smooth leadership transition), statistics suggest that a healthy, planned transition led by the outgoing leader places the organization in the best position to win.

---

[3] Management Sciences for Health, "Planning for Leadership Transition," *The Manager* (Boston), vol. 10, no. 1 (2001): 1-22.

One way to foster healthy transitions is to lead focus groups with the stakeholders, who may be members of the church congregation, students in the seminary, members of the staff, funding sources, boards, and committees. Fostering conversations that broaden the understanding of the culture of the organization, its traditions, history, and values will enhance the process. Helping the organization to analyze its current position and future needs is another way to lead in the transition. Gathering crucial organizational materials in one place is also helpful to the process. And, depending on the relationship with the organization, the outgoing leader may be extremely helpful in identifying the next leader, even to the point of naming her or his successor.

One author suggests that perhaps the greatest benefit an outgoing leader can give to an organization, especially if she or he is highly loved and respected, is the affirmation of the incoming leader. For indeed, "his or her approval of the incoming leader means more than the résumé, gifts, and abilities of the incoming leader."[4] This affirmation cannot only serve to set the mind of the incoming leader at ease, but it can also calm the inevitable anxieties of the stakeholders in the organization. This is the exact gift that the revered leader Moses gave to his successor Joshua. In the sight of all of the people of Israel, Moses gave this admonition to Joshua, "Be strong and of good courage, for you must go with this people to the land which the Lord has sworn to their fathers to give them, and you shall cause them to inherit it. And the Lord, He is the One who goes before you" (Deuteronomy 31:7-8). Moses's example, and the ensuing success of Joshua's leadership, suggests that the leadership transition "must include the public affirmation of the incoming leader in order for the transition to have a chance at being successful."[5]

As a member of a relay team in track and field, this writer has both received and given affirmation, cheers and vocal advocacy in the baton passing maneuver. For, while the passing of the baton is principal, the win is paramount. Regardless of how far the former runner has advanced the team, the race is not over until the mission is accomplished. The next

---

[4] Marvin Anthony Moss, *Next: Surviving A Leadership Transition* (Nashville: Abingdon Press, 2013), Kindle Electronic Edition: Location 326-35.

[5] Ibid., 336.

runner must take the baton and run successfully. Moses must release confidently. Joshua must increase courageously. Yet, we must not miss the fact that Joshua obviously needed reassurance about his ability to handle the new role of senior leadership. The need to have this constant reassurance at the beginning of his tenure may give us some clues about the challenges that new leaders face, especially if they succeed an iconic leader. Thus, we will now examine the various issues and concerns of the incoming leader.

A group of leaders was asked to rank a list of life's challenges in order of difficulty. Much to the surprise of the surveyors, making a leadership transition was ranked number one most frequently by the participants and appeared in the top three answers on everyone's list. This type of transition outranked such life challenges as dealing with death, divorce and other devastating situations that often make a list of such nature when presented to others. A promotion within the organization was the reason for the leadership change for most of the respondents. While the promotion was accompanied by a sense of advancement and accomplishment, and was definitely viewed as positive, the majority of those surveyed emphasized the immense stress that accompanied the transition.[6] Exploring these stress factors may foster a greater understanding of the transition process and give helpful tools to those who initiate, execute and participate in leadership transitions, particularly as related to those who are promoted to higher levels of leadership within an organization. These tools may in fact be transferred and applied to a wide variety of leadership transition venues, including those occurring within a church setting.

The term "culture shock" might best describe the transition experience of those people who responded to the study referenced above and is even applicable to the experiences of the writer of this paper and of others with whom this writer is personally familiar. While most applications of this phenomenon are for those who travel to a foreign country, culture shock, by definition, may relate to life crises in a

---

[6] Matt Paese and Richard S. Wellins, "Leaders in Transition: Stepping Up, Not Off," Development Dimensions International, Inc. (2007), 1-22, accessed March 22, 2014, http://www.ddiworld.com.

variety of other areas. Paul Pedersen contends that a person undergoing a significant change of any type in life may experience a process of adaptation or accommodation that is equivalent to the conditions described as culture shock.[7]

Pederson suggests that culture shock can come to any person who encounters unfamiliar events and unexpected circumstances in his or her life. He lists five stages of culture shock through which a person may navigate when experiencing these significant changes in life. His list is based on the work of Peter Adler and others:

1. **Honeymoon Stage**, which is characterized by excitement and anticipation.

2. **Disintegration Stage** brings a sense of being overwhelmed and inadequate.

3. **Reintegration Stage** increases confidence but still carries some questions as to why he or she ever accepted the change in the first place, idealizing the old place.

4. **Autonomy Stage**, the individual acquires a more balanced perspective.

5. **Interdependence Stage**, the individual begins to feel more comfortable and capable. There is now a feeling of being "at home."[8]

One might expect that the phenomenon of culture shock and the associated stages therewith might be diminished and perhaps shortened for a long-term member of an organization who rises to a higher place of leadership. The assumption is that the familiarity with the organization and its stakeholders would give this person an advantage because he or she is still essentially at home. However, that assumption was clearly unsubstantiated by the experiences of many individuals whose stories were cited in several case studies. Indeed, one publication implied that

---

[7] Paul Pedersen, *The Five Stages of Culture Shock: Critical Incidents Around the World* (Westport: Greenwood Press, 1995), 1.

[8] Ibid., 3.

a person rising from within an organization may experience culture shock to a greater degree because the view is so different within an organization with which she or he had been so long affiliated. It is a different world. New skills are required because the upward transition decreases the opportunity for the direct hands-on applications that were normal at the previous level and requires a greater capacity to strategize, to work through others and to keep balance in the political network of the organization. The learning curve can be steep.

Ascending through the ranks certainly has its benefits to ensure organizational stability, but it necessitates a shifting of time investment for the promoted leader. Communicating, planning, building a team, strategizing and influencing were five key areas in which the investment of time shifted after a promotion was received as cited by respondents to a leadership survey. These skills were not always required or were utilized much less frequently at the former position. Many found that the skills acquired at the previous level did not fully transfer, nor did they adequately address the dynamics of the newly occupied place of leadership. Upon reflection, the majority of the respondents indicated that having a clearly defined process that included a period of mentoring and coaching from the former leader — prior to and following the promotion — as well as more definitive involvement of the Board of Directors — may have helped decrease the level of culture shock experienced as a result of the promotion.[9]

Frankly, the writer of this article appreciates the opportunity to define "officially" the emotions and concerns that can accompany a promotion, even one for which the person senses a godly calling. Even smooth transitions have rocky places. Godly places have accompanying problems. The "Honeymoon Stage," in which change is idealized, will give way to the "Disintegration Stage," in which change is demonized. But, because nothing will last forever, this stage, if one hangs around and remains creative, will yield to the "Interdependence Stage," at which one knows for certain that she or he is the called and confirmed leader and is once again, "at home." Having personally experienced the awesome destiny of following an iconic leader, the writer can assert with assurance

---

[9] Pedersen, 7.

that the healthy process of transition, while it cannot mediate against the culture shock, can help to make the navigation through the stages purposeful.

What then is needed when it is time to leave? The following transition process is suggested by this writer.

1. **Learning.** The current leader, whenever possible and feasible, must initiate a process of learning that includes knowing when to leave, knowing when to talk about leaving, and knowing how to lead the stakeholders in the conversation. Why? This leader holds the baton.

2. **Legacy Honoring.** The incoming leader must honor the strengths of the outgoing leader and of the organization. No relay runner turns around and runs back to the starting line to prove his or her abilities. No one comes to an existing place that does not already have existing strengths. Find them and celebrate them, openly.

3. **Leaving the Past.** While no runner seeks to negate the progress of the previous runner by dishonoring the starting point, the previous runner does not continue to run past the handoff zone. Yes, there is a necessary overlap of the old and the new. But, there is a time when the old must decrease so that the new can increase. Wise is the leader who knows the timing of such.

4. **Leading the Future.** The focus must be on ministry or it will yield to a mess; on mission or it will yield to madness. Take the baton and run to the finish line.

Dean Sebastian has demonstrated great skills on both sides of the leading and leaving cycle. His modeling of how to manage transitions will prove helpful to the various types of institutions in which he has served as they continue to experience necessary endings. With great courage, tenacity, and skillfulness, this Ambassador Sebastian has shown us all what to do when it's time to leave.

Looking Back and Moving Forward: Memories and More

Arlo F. Newell

Christian leadership is qualified by the admiration and cooperation of those who follow. Without followers there would be no leader. The significant success of higher education in the Church of God reveals successive leadership uniting the Church and Academy. From its beginning, Anderson University and the Church of God have merged spiritual and intellectual development, exemplified in the lives of leaders called of God, accepted by the Church, and inspired by the Holy Spirit. Maintaining balance between individual ardor and communal order, they have developed programs and established institutions to fulfill the high calling which God has placed upon his people (Eph. 4:1). Such positive and effective leadership is open to being examined or evaluated by scripture, Christian tradition, and contemporary knowledge. Leaders are learners; they remain teachable.

The comments herein should not be taken as judgmental nor laudatory but rather as the observations of a pastor-preacher, one who has walked with you and prayed for you through the last half century. My objective is to approach the assignment from four periods of time as we have traveled this road less traveled. All four will have some relevance to the divine call upon our lives and ministry. As we remember leaders, institutions, programs and/or ministries, let us seek to determine the extent of their motivation, the depth of their commitment and the quality of their spiritual integrity. Looking through these lenses, let us remember the historical, personal, developmental and generational times of our lives.

Foundational — Spiritual

Historical evidence reveals that the emergence, development, and sustenance of a movement or institution are in direct proportion to the motivation of the leader. That with which we have been entrusted is the result of pioneers, men and women of faith motivated by their passion for biblical truth. From different faith backgrounds they were drawn together as the Holy Spirit imparted scriptural understanding. There were no visions of churches or education facilities, only an unquenchable thirst for Bible truth.

Church historian John W. V. Smith wrote about this as the foundational beginning of what we have received. Of the year 1878 he wrote, "one of the chief points among the pioneers was this desire to preach all the truth of the Gospel of Christ."[1] Gilbert Stafford wrote, "Historically, the assumption among us has always been when we go to church we go to receive further biblical instruction."[2]

Commitment to this "all truth" concept was indicated by our pioneers' willingness to leave other religious bodies, separating themselves from those who were not open to all of Scripture. D. S. Warner, because of his vision of truth, willingly left the ordination he had received. Others, in seeking to give financial support, sold property and possessions, referring to Acts 2:44-45. Belief determines action (James 2:17), and having received this truth, they sought to follow the example of Christ (Matthew 5:1) and began to study and to teach. Being commissioned to "go and preach" (Mark 16:15) inspired them to preach, teach, and publish. There were no training schools but where a need was made known, teachers emerged.

In seminal form, this was the beginning of on-the-job training, meeting a need and equipping the church. Leadership evolved not because individuals were self-seeking or power-hungry but because they sought to serve — true servant leaders.

---

[1] John W.V. Smith, *I Will Build My Church: Biblical Insights on Distinguishing Doctrines of the Church of God* (Anderson, Ind.: Warner Press, 1985), 35.

[2] Gilbert W. Stafford, *Church of God at the Crossroads* (Anderson, Ind.: Warner Press, 2000), 60.

The Good News was published in the Gospel Trumpet on a hand operated press in D. S. Warner's kitchen and distributed free. After this humble beginning and in different locations, the Trumpet operation settled in Anderson, Ind., in 1905.

Through the pages of the Gospel Trumpet, the seed was being planted and young minds were attracted to this truth. From Kansas in 1907, Otto F. Linn heard the call, and leaving the chicken farm, moved to Anderson to be a part of this community of faith. In 1916, Adam W. Miller, a young man from the Baltimore area wrote asking, "When is something going to be provided for young ministers training for gospel work?"

With needs being expressed and questions being asked, those who had first been followers now became leaders. J. T. Wilson, a true visionary, was the new president of the Gospel Trumpet and had initiated Bible studies in the Trumpet Home. Gradually some organization was being accepted in the Movement. With requests from the field, action was taken and a committee appointed to proceed in launching a school. J. T. Wilson, R. R. Byrum, F. G. Smith, H. A. Sherwood, and J. E. Campbell served on the committee. Leadership requirements were outlined in Acts 6:2-3, 7: character, spirit-filled wisdom (sanctified common sense) and faith. The first sign ever posted in front of Old Main revealed the development of the fledgling enterprise: ANDERSON BIBLE TRAINING SCHOOL AND SEMINARY.

In Oct. of 1917, with only a few students, willing though untrained instructors and little financial backing but a firm foundation, the school opened. As president of the Gospel Trumpet Company and chairman of the original committee appointed to develop this new school, Wilson was selected by the group as the first principal of the school housed in the Trumpet Home.

Immediately, Wilson began searching for responsible leadership to serve in this noble purpose. With no job description, it was desired that the person selected would have both theological and educational experience. Having never met John Morrison, he wrote, asking him to give consideration to serving as the principal of this Training School. With little formal education, his credentials only his commitment to Christ and to the Church, plus his integrity, honesty, and maturity, John Morrison was invited to serve as principal and accepted.

After 12 years in that office, experiencing both blessings and curses, Morrison would write in the Gospel Trumpet, "If we hope to save our young people from the shipwreck of faith during the process of their education, we as a church must make it possible for them to receive that education amid Christian environments."[3]

Personal — Relational

The first 25 years of Anderson Bible Training School (ABTS) reveal the struggle for survival and the dedication of "dream catchers" who laid hold onto the dream and pursued it with passion. Though recorded in history, it has also become the personal experience of many still living today people with whom we are related or with whom we have served as servant-leaders in the Kingdom. The depression of the late 1920s and the poverty of the mid-1930s called for leaders to manage money when there was no money. It is at such times that leadership is stripped of popularity, position, power, or prestige. For those who dug the footings and poured the foundations, these were days of discipline, dedication and determination. They believed in the relationship of body, mind and spirit.

Leaders produce leaders. The model is as old as Scripture. Jesus called his disciples to follow him. Paul counseled Timothy, "the things you have learned of me . . . commit to trustworthy men who will be competent to teach others also" (II Timothy 2:2).

Within 20 years of the first graduating class of ABTS, teachers and pastors were serving across the nation. Samuel and Eleanor (Schlabaugh) Dooty, my first pastors, were members of the Class of '23. They were co-pastors in Hutchinson, Kan., and inspired a group of leaders: Nellie (Fields) Snowden, Phillip Kinley, Ralph Little, and Ed Baize. Not all were preachers; many were educators and professional business leaders. Already the leaders of ABTS were sensing the need for a liberal arts college to meet the needs of the whole world with the whole gospel. They believed that biblical truth was not only spiritual but also intellectual,

---

[3] Barry L. Callen, *Enriching Mind and Spirit: A History of Higher Education in the Church of God* (Anderson) (Anderson, Ind.: Anderson University Press, 2007), 46.

impacting the totality of one's personality. "Be not conformed to this world but be transformed by the renewing of your mind" (Romans 12:2). The truth, when "rightly divided" (II Timothy 2:15), directs us to "the mind of Christ" (Phil. 2:5), and we are to "think on these things" (Phil. 4:8).

Increased enrollment was the result of the integrity and character of those leading the institution. Rather than new buildings or scholarships, students were attracted to ABTS by subjects being taught by faculty who believed what they were teaching. It was the leadership principle found in scripture: "The word became flesh . . . dwelt with us . . . and we understood grace and truth" (John 1:14).

A contributing factor in building relationships at ABTS was Old Main as the focal point of all campus activities. Though sometimes limited in space, it was accessible and functional. Housed in one building were administration offices, classrooms, faculty offices, library, biology laboratory, kitchen and dining room, and the women's dormitory. Many of the rooms served for duplicate activities as needed. With increased enrollment and expanded course offerings, growth would be limited without additional space and financial support.

As visionary leaders, the administration had developed and maintained strong relationships with the general agencies of the church. It was the church that gave birth to the young Bible school and therefore openly shared when called on to do so. When a gymnasium was needed, the original 1907 tabernacle was put into service. With the enrollment of men overflowing, the old camp meeting dormitory was transformed into the "barnatory" or men's dormitory. What had previously been a home for retired ministers and/or missionaries was transformed into East Hall, a women's dormitory. When graduation time arrived and the church could not hold the crowd, the old wooden tabernacle was pressed into service.

This relationship between ABTS and the Church of God gave meaning to the truth of unity. While not agreeing totally on all issues of faith and practice, the personal relationship of key leaders of ABTS and the church strengthened each other. Barry Callen would record the words of Robert Reardon: "I believe that Anderson College's current health is derived from its profound commitment as a functioning part of the life of the Church of God . . . For the university to fulfill its future destiny, this covenant relationship between campus and church must never be abandoned."[4]

Developmental — Theological

From its beginning on that October day in 1917, the seed had been planted. Anderson Bible Training School and Seminary: the very name carried with it the intent of those committed leaders. Seminary is defined as "theological training for ministers." In its development they were on course — first, Bible training, approval by the ministerial assembly, then acceptance of being a church-related liberal arts college.

By 1932 the first liberal arts graduating class received their degrees. Soon thereafter, some of the ministerial students would enroll at established seminaries for further training. History reveals that "Undergraduate study in Bible and religion stimulated a hunger for advanced theological study . . . [and] it was Oberlin Seminary in Ohio that became the school of choice"[5] of many of our graduates. Therefore it was no surprise when there was the cry, "We want our own seminary." By 1947 there emerged a five-year course of study for graduates. W. Dale Oldham, Adam Miller, Russell Olt, C. Lowry Quinn, and John Kane submitted the plan.[6]

In the dark years of 1946-47, when Dr. Morrison was physically incapable to serve, his desire to move the young school ahead was not hindered. Accompanied by Russell Olt and Robert Reardon, they pressed forward in launching the School of Theology. To justify their action they informed the church, "We have received repeated and insistent requests

---

[4] Barry L. Callen, Faith, *Learning & Life: Views from the President's Office of Anderson University* (Anderson, Ind.: Anderson University and Warner Press, 1991) 157.

[5] Merle D. Strege, *I Saw the Church: The Life of the Church of God Told Theologically* (Anderson, Ind.: Warner Press, 2002), 235.

[6] Barry L. Callen, *Guide of Soul and Mind: The Story of Anderson University* (Anderson, Ind.: Warner Press, 1992), 147.

of ministers on the field."[7] Otto F. Linn, Adam Miller and several others supported this move. To clarify any questions from the church, they justified their action with this announcement: "On the campus of Anderson College and Theological Seminary . . . the training will be especially designed to fit our students for the pastoral, evangelistic, religious education, and other fields of activity in the Church of God."[8]

Tom Brokaw referred to this period of history as The Greatest Generation. He was not referring to the church but certainly these Church of God leaders qualify as being counted among those who reflect the greatness of godliness.

The School of Theology first opened its doors in October of 1950. The crowded conditions of Old Main and the lack of other facilities left no option: the SOT would meet in an upper room of Old Main with Dr. Earl Martin as the first dean and Gene Newberry as the only full-time professor. It would be 1961 before the School of Theology building came into view.

The task before them in the beginning was difficult and demanding. Now there was the challenge of building a seminary library, selecting and recruiting a faculty, developing courses to be offered, enrolling students, and raising funds. It was a daunting assignment and required leadership with great dedication.

Those who have served exemplify what one writer has called "grace-full leadership": "Christian Leadership is fundamentally different from all other leadership. Even if the organization looks like a secular organization, there is still a difference . . . for God's Spirit is at work in the heart and life of a grace-full life."[9] The School of Theology has been blessed by such spiritually qualified leaders:

1950-1953   Earl L. Martin

1953-1962   Adam W. Miller

1962-1974   Gene W. Miller

---

[7] Ibid., 156.

[8] Ibid., 158.

[9] John C. Bowling, *Grace-Full Leadership: Understanding the Heart of a Christian Leader* (Kansas City, Mo.: Beacon Hill Press of Kansas City, 2011), 9.

1974-1983   Barry L. Callen

1983-1988   Jerry C. Grubbs

1989-1995   James Earl Massey

1995-2014   David L. Sebastian

I have been privileged to know each of these leaders personally. Their ministry of Christian leadership has demonstrated the spirit of servanthood that motivated them, evidenced by their commitment and supported by Christian integrity. Truly they have revealed what William Willimon calls "a will to lead and the grace to follow."[10]

Due to health conditions, Dr. Earl Martin served as dean for only three years. However, his leadership set the spiritual tone of the school for the future. As professor of theology at Anderson College, he had instilled within us an understanding of the Word and a desire to know more. His major writing, *Toward Understanding God,* which Church of God historian Merle Strege calls Dr. Martin's magnum opus,[11] points the reader to seek to know God through the Word. Rather than easy answers to difficult questions, he encourages the reader to discover God experientially, to know him personally. Each Dean made a unique contribution of leadership. These years have been a testimony to the unity experienced through diversity. With humility they have washed feet, served communion, wept with students, and survived storms. The School of Theology is not a business; it is neither a church nor a political machine. It requires Christian leadership strengthened by the Holy Spirit.

Generational — Missional

"I have a goodly heritage, my future is bright!" (Psalm 16:16 CEV). The Psalms speak directly to the realities of life. My first introduction to this particular verse came from Dr. Carl Kardatzke. Two years before

---

[10] William H. Willimon and Bryan Langlands, *A Will to Lead and the Grace to Follow: Letters on Leadership from a Peculiar Prophet* (Nashville: Abingdon Press, 2011), ix.

[11] Strege, 252.

I was born, he graduated from ABTS. As a young man, this verse had given to him an awareness of what he had received from those who lived before him. He reminded me of this as we discussed my future. He became my mentor and his influence has followed me to this 88th year of my pilgrimage. The "goodly heritage" which he had received was passed on to the next generation.

Now, the question is, "What legacy will we pass on to succeeding generations? Will those who come behind us find us to have been faithful? Will the fire of our devotion light the way?" If we fail to plan for the future, we tend to react to circumstances rather than exercise decisive leadership. God has a plan and a purpose (Jeremiah 29:11), and he will lead if we will follow.

We have been given much as stewards and are accountable not only for how we have used that which we received, but also for how we pass it on to generations yet unborn. More than buildings and accreditation, we have received eternal truth from ethical leaders, with integrity, maturity, humility, and leadership ability. With consistent discipline they have exemplified conduct above reproach: positive not negative, humble not boastful, spiritual and moral, relational not political.

Henri J. M. Nouwen wrote, "Christian leadership in the future is not a leadership of power and control, but a leadership of powerlessness and humility in which the suffering Servant of God, Jesus Christ, is made known... Real maturity is not in control but in the willingness to be led where you would not go"[12] (Note: Phil.2:5-8). Leaders do not possess authority; they only express the authority of the gospel — authority shaped by the gospel. Leadership is a position of privilege: it is a privilege to serve and to say with the Psalmist, "Even when I am old and gray, do not forsake me, O God, till I declare your power to the next generation, your might to all who are to come" (Psalm 71:18).

Mission statements are an attempt on the part of organizations to state clearly and publicly what their purpose is. A missional church is one that knows the reason for its existence and what it seeks to accomplish. In the

---

[12] Henri J. M. Nouwen, *In the Name of Jesus: Reflections on Christian Leadership* (New York: Crossroad, 1989), 82.

2014 *Yearbook of the Church of God,* the mission statements of these two institutions are clearly stated:

> The mission of Anderson University is to educate for a life of faith and service in the church and society.[13]

> The mission of Anderson University School of Theology is to form women and men for the ministry of biblical reconciliation.[14]

Though stated differently from the past, the intent of both statements remains the same. Inherent in the wording, one finds the spirit of the Great Commandment (Matthew 22:37-39), and the outreach of the Great Commission (Matthew 28:19-20). By putting the Missions Statements in print, the public knows that "we are ambassadors for Christ, ministers of reconciliation" (II Corinthians 5:20) as we educate for service.

Leadership continues to be consistent and committed to that for which we were established. There is a trust that develops when we remain theologically grounded. A young pastor wrote to me recently about the doctrinal teachings of the Church: "I don't want to go back to the pioneer days, but I do wish to regain some of their devotion and key truths that they believed in and suffered for." With the cultural shifts which have taken place theologically, there is need for intelligent, inspired preaching and teaching. Dr. Walter Brueggemann comments that with "the deepening crisis of the church in the U.S. society . . . the minister must be as well schooled as possible."[15] We endeavor to educate and form persons of faith for today, a faith that is personal, scriptural and practical. Theology is more than theoretical; it is experiential. Beyond the printed page there is the Christ: the way, the truth, the life (John 14:6).

Before Paul wrote about being called ministers of reconciliation he had written:

---

[13] Stephen R. Lewis, Managing Editor, *2014 Yearbook: United States and Canada* (Anderson, Ind.: Warner Press, 2014), 29.

[14] Ibid., 30.

[15] Walter Brueggemann, *The Word Militant: Preaching a Decentering Word* (Minneapolis: Fortress Press, 2010), x.

When I came to you, I did not come with eloquence or superior wisdom as I proclaimed to you the testimony about God. For I resolved to know nothing while I was with you except Jesus Christ and him crucified. I came to you in weakness and fear, and with much trembling. My message and my preaching were not with wise and persuasive words, but with a demonstration of the Spirit's power, so that your faith might not rest on men's wisdom, but on God's power" (I Corinthians 2:1-5 NIV).

"Go make disciples" is our mission as we teach and preach the Gospel. Dr. George Buttrick, the gifted preacher, author, and teacher was given a very elaborate introduction before speaking. His first comment when at the pulpit was, "There are no great preachers; there is only a great Gospel."[16]

Beyond the Horizon

"We stand today upon the shore but beyond the horizon there is more and more."
Unrealistic expectations or visions can become the seedbed of depression.
"Faith gives substance to our hopes and makes us
certain of realities we do not see."
(Hebrews 11:1 NEB)

Challenged by a changing culture and a transitional time in leadership in the university and the church, we have the opportunity to exercise faith and trust in the God of the future. Let us...

• CONFESS our faith in God, in his revealed Word, and the church for which Christ died. Our hope is built on nothing less.

• REAFFIRM our covenant relationship between the Church of God and Anderson University. We are interdependent and we really do need each other.

---

[16] Quoted in Kenneth C Kinghorn, *A Celebration of Ministry: Essays in Honor of Frank Bateman Stanger* (Wilmore, Ky.: Francis Asbury Publishing Company, 1982), 19.

- ACCEPT the challenge of change as we exhibit the wisdom to know what not to change; some truths are non-negotiable.

- EMBRACE the benefits of this high-tech culture by being creative and innovative. Make use of technology as we equip faculty and students in the fulfillment of our mission.

- EXPLORE the possibility of expanding and extending our ministry through extension programs for mission stations, a global concept.

- DEVELOP a financial support system that will enable students to graduate debt free. Scholarships, endowments, special gifts, and/ or congregational student support.

- ESTABLISH a forum for addressing the social issues of the day. Be prophetic in applying God's Word to violence, STD, poverty, war abuse in the church and world, political corruption.

Rise up, O Church of God!
Have done with lesser things,
Give heart and soul and mind and strength
To serve the King of Kings.

Additional reading resources:

Due to limitations of the length of the paper, it was impossible to include quotations or insights gained from the following. I recommend them for those who would read more on this related subject of academic development for discipleship:

Discipline: Sören Kierkegaard, *Purity of Heart is to Will One Thing*. Radford, Va.: A & D Publishing, 2008.

Servant Leadership: James R. Hawkinson and Robert K. Johnston, *Servant Leadership*. Chicago: Covenant Pub., 1993 (two volumes).

Preaching: Albert Mohler, *He is not Silent: Preaching in a Postmodern World*. Chicago: Moody Publishers, 2008.

HOLY CALLING, HOLY LEADERSHIP: LEADERSHIP IN THE LIFE OF SEMINARIES

David L. Neidert

Seminaries are big business. According to the Association of Theological Schools, seminaries "collectively spend about $1.8 billion to educate its students... with a collective net tuition income of $466 million."[1] They also have significant dollars in endowment with "$6.95 billion in cash and investments."[2] To gain some perspective on what this means, Arizona State University, the United States' largest university by headcount, "spends about $1.6 billion to educate its students in its multicampus system" and has cash and investments of "only $0.72 billion" comparatively.[3] Seminaries are big business.

On paper, seminaries look like any other business enterprise. They are comprised of boards and administrative staff, utilize marketing plans and balance sheets, manage payrolls and information technology departments, and much more. They calculate net revenues, consistently engage in cost analysis, and spend considerable time reviewing and strategizing about projected revenues against expenses in future years. They also work diligently to raise capital for improvements, programs, and new construction to benefit or attract students or guests who might utilize their campuses.

---

[1] Greg Henson and Gary Hoag, "More Schools, Fewer Students: What's your seminary's position in the changing market of theological education?," *In Trust: Center for Theological Schools 25,* no. 1, (Autumn 2013): 13.

[2] Ibid.

[3] Ibid. See the ranking of Arizona State University since 2009, which provides collected information from university websites or educational data available for the top ten schools. Wikipedia List of United States university campuses by enrollment http://en.wikipedia.org/wiki/List_of_United_States_university_campuses_by_enrollment (Accessed 1/27/2014).

If seminaries were merely a mirror of other business enterprises, identifying leadership talent for them would simply be a matter of accessing an individual's past successes, employment track record, or demonstrated skills to oversee cost containment, investment strategies, or resource development.[4]

But seminaries are not another category of big business. They are a part of Kingdom work. While forgotten at times in the search for headcounts, endowment dollars, and staffing needs, seminaries serve as places for equipping disciples for ministry; for giving "the church and the world women and men who have experienced, through the process of quality teaching-learning, the transforming power of the gospel."[5] While seminaries do need leaders who are competent in business practices, they must also be guided by those who understand their responsibility as a holy vocation.[6] Leadership in seminaries cannot ultimately be about return-on-investment, growing headcounts or physical plant, or the reputation of the school academically, as important as these measurements are for assessing quality. Seminary leaders must work out of a holy calling, so that the institutions they guide might in the end be acknowledged more heavily for contributing to Kingdom work, as expressed in Matthew 28:18-20, than the size of the school, its endowment, or reputation in this world.

Seminary leaders must possess a heart committed to God, his Kingdom work, and his plan for humankind. With this commitment, holy

---

[4] As a former human resource director, these are the baseline for determining a person's candidacy for a position, whether entry level or management.

[5] Gordon T. Smith, *Called to Be Saints: An Invitation to Christian Maturity* (Downer's Grove, Illinois: Intervarsity Press, 2014), p 220. Smith's book provides an excellent treatment of this topic. His Appendix B, "Christian Higher Education," challenges Christian institutions, including seminaries, to remember their work with students is about "transformation in Christ" and then helping students see their responsibility in living out that change vocationally. pp 213-250.

[6] Holiness, for this paper, is defined as "consecration to the Lord and his service." This holiness does not come from the leader and one's moral development, but is the character of Christ abiding in the person through the Holy Spirit. R.A. Finalyson, "Holiness, Holy," in *New Bible Dictionary,* ed. JD Douglas, (Wheaton, Illinois: Tyndale, 1984), 487.

leadership will then appropriately cultivate spiritual elements necessary for furthering the Kingdom, not just skills for running a big business.

Seminary leaders who acknowledge their role as a holy calling should embody at least some foundational characteristics as they daily engage with faculty, staff, students, and the wider body of the church. These characteristics are an observable personal faith and confession, spiritual disciplines, discernment, and servanthood.[7]

Personal Faith and Confession

The classic books on leadership start mostly in the same place: leaders have a mission or sense of purpose.[8] It is important that leaders have a personal mission or identified life purpose in order to lead passionately, whether in an organization or in the many spheres of life. While those who would lead in seminaries may have a stated personal mission or purpose, it must ultimately rest in the person of Jesus Christ as Lord and Savior. Holy leadership is grounded first and foremost in one's relationship with Christ. That confession is critical for guiding the leader's personal self-awareness, role, activities, discernment, and responsibilities for the Kingdom work of seminaries. Whatever leaders

---

[7] While I have been reading, studying, teaching, and writing about leadership since 1987 from the broad field as well as those authors focused specifically on business, I am also influenced by my years of reading spiritual classics and recent scholarship in this area. I recommend books by Eugene Peterson, *Under the Unpredictable Plant: An Exploration in Vocational Holiness,* Grand Rapids, Michigan: William B. Eerdmans, 1992; Gordon T. Smith's works, *The Voice of Jesus: Discernment, Prayer, and the Witness of the Spirit,* Downer's Grove, Illinois: Intervarsity Press, 2003 and *Called to be Saints: An Invitation to Christian Maturity,* Downer's Grove, Illinois: Intervarsity Press, 2014; Dennis Kinlaw, *Let's Start with Jesus: A New Way of Doing Theology,* Grand Rapids, Michigan: Zondervan, 2005; the many books of Henri Nouwen as well as Dietrich Bonhoeffer, CS Lewis, and Christian writers of the 14th through 16th centuries of the church. The characteristics I present here are by no means exhaustive, but highlight a life-style deeply grafted into Christ (cf. John 15).

[8] See the works by Warren Bennis, Peter Drucker, Barry Posner and James Kouzes, Robert Greenleaf, Max DePree, Frances Hesslebein, among many others.

---

do, it is viewed through the life, death, resurrection, and relationship one has with Christ.

A personal and professed identification and abiding with Christ centers and helps the leader see his or her work within a seminary, not as big business, but as fundamentally Kingdom work. J. B. Torrance is helpful here by intimating that confession of Christ as Lord of our lives defines our allegiance with him thereby acknowledging that the work we do is of his Kingdom and receives life only in and through him. But at the same time, our confession of Christ as our Lord reminds us we are limited, that we have the potential of allowing our egos and fleshly desires to hijack our leadership (and decisions) instead of leaning on God's grace to show us what is true and right.[9] In considering why this confession is so important, Eugene Peterson warns, "There are a thousand ways of being religious without submitting to Christ's lordship, and people are practiced in most of them."[10] Personal and public confession of Jesus as Lord anchors the leader. Without it, leaders can easily and unintentionally slide into directing a non-descript educational organization focused solely on the outcomes of good business instead of guiding a Christian learning community focused on equipping and transforming disciples for Kingdom work.

Spiritual Disciplines

If the seminary's role in Kingdom work focuses on equipping and transforming disciples (i.e. students) then those who lead must be exemplars of living a transformed life. Seminaries talk often about spiritual formation and require students to take such courses as a means of maturing as disciples and future ministers of the gospel. If seminaries, then, require this pilgrimage of students (which may include both the

---

[9] J. B. Torrance, "Confession," in *New Bible Dictionary,* ed. JD Douglas, (Wheaton, Illinois: Tyndale, 1984), 224-225.

[10] Eugene Peterson, *Under the Unpredictable Plant: An Exploration in Vocational Holiness,* (Grand Rapids, Michigan: William B. Eerdmans, 1992), 84.

study and practice of disciplines), holy leadership must also practice spiritual disciplines essential for transformed lives. As Richard Foster writes, "The Disciplines allow us to place ourselves before God so that He can transform us."[11]

Foster and others give attention to spiritual disciplines such as meditation, fasting, study, simplicity, solitude, service, and prayer.[12] These practices have proven essential to Christians for the past 2,000 years and are receiving resurgence in the postmodern world.[13] While space does not permit examining each of the disciplines and its contribution to holy leadership, it is essential to speak about prayer, as it will also relate to the next characteristic of discernment.

Returning to Foster, he writes, "Prayer is the central avenue God uses to transform us . . . Progressively (through prayer) we are taught to see things from His point of view."[14] Prayer cannot be relegated to the here-and-there moments of our days. Prayer is a time holy leadership

---

[11] Richard J. Foster, *Celebration of Discipline: The Path of Spiritual Growth,* (New York: Harper & Row, Publishers, 1978), 6. Foster is right in this exhortation. Those involved in the academy have a tendency to work diligently at increasing the capacity of scholarship. While this is essential and virtuous, it is easy to neglect the spiritual life for the cerebral life. As Foster warns, "The desperate need today is not for a greater number of intelligent people, or gifted people, but for deep people." p 1.

[12] Foster's *Celebration of Discipline* provides a list via his chapters, while others embed them throughout their writings, such as Ignatius of Loyola, Aquinas, Thomas Keating, Henri Nouwen, Thomas Merton, and others.

[13] One of the best recent books I have encountered is Jamin Goggin and Kyle Strobe, editors, *Reading the Christian Classics: a Guide for Evangelicals,* Downer's Grove, Illinois: Intervarsity Press, 2013. The book helps evangelicals to understand the value of the Christian classics, as well as being aware of the vast differences between these writings and evangelicalism. One of the most important sections calls attention to Eastern Orthodox writings and the difficulties evangelicals will encounter if they do not understand the background of this religious heritage. I recommend Andrew Louth, *Introducing Eastern Orthodox Theology,* Downer's Grove, Illinois: Intervarsity Press, 2013 as an introduction.

[14] Foster, 30.

marks and carves out with intention because through it, leaders establish, nurture, and move into the life of union with Christ. In prayer, the leader desires to learn about and from, listen to and obey, and experience the God who transforms by permitting one to understand themselves in light of grace, mercy, forgiveness, and love. While the adage that "God changes things" may be true, it is more important that leaders come to long for how God changes us – *so that* leaders might appropriately, courageously, and strategically know the difference between whether one's leadership is geared toward constructing edifices to academia and stroking personal ego or whether it is guiding a specialized faith community toward spiritual maturity, equipping and transforming lives that glorify God above all else.

Constant, intentional prayer helps the leader to know the mind of Christ. And it is in knowing God's ways through the power of the Spirit that holy leadership can discern the proper, good, and right courses of actions for the educational institutions they direct.

Discernment

Discernment and prayer are linked. The Christian classics, as well as more recent writings, demonstrate this connection. The progression we can identify in these classics seems to be that the more one spends time in prayer, the deeper their relationship develops with God, who gives insight to the disciple through the power of the Holy Spirit for the glory of God and his Kingdom. It is as Jesus shares with the disciples, "When the Spirit of truth comes, he will guide you into all the truth; for he will not speak on his own, but will speak whatever he hears, and he will declare to you the things that are to come. He will glorify me, because he will take what is mine and declare it to you" (John 15:13-14, NRSV). Smith reminds us of this connection between prayer and discernment. God does not just give us wisdom or discernment, but "it (wisdom) is formed through personal encounter . . . Through the discipline of prayer we nurture a receptivity to God," and thus "learn to see reality more clearly, understand our circumstances and appropriate afresh the grace to respond with integrity and freedom to our circumstances and to the people with who we live and work."[15]

While prayer is critical for holy leadership personally, it is also the life blood of the seminary community. If seminaries are to engage learners effectively in this mission of transformation, the community must also pray and discern together when initiating mission, structures, curricular design, or programmatic endeavors. As Kathleen Cahalan reminds us, "Christian discernment is a communal, not a solo, practice. It occurs in

---

[15] Gordon T. Smith, *The Voice of Jesus: Discernment, Prayer and the Witness of the Spirit,* (Downer's Grove, Illinois: Intervarsity Press, 2003), 161-162. Smith's book makes the significant link between prayer and discernment in the chapter, The Character of our Prayers, 157-182. James Orr and William Walther provide excellent commentary on this insight related to discernment from 1 Corinthians 2:14-16. In discussing this relationship in Christ and the wisdom available through the Spirit, they write, "The *affairs of God's spirit* include the insights about the meaning of the gospel and, as the sequel seems to indicate, the application of the spirit of the gospel to all problematic areas of life." They move further by saying because of a person's connection with God through the Spirit, which is a central part of the "Christian fellowship," that "the spiritual person is capable of evaluating properly the good and evil (he or she) confronts, of estimating what things are worth while and what things are not." William F. Orr and James Arthur Walther, 1 Corinthians, in *The Anchor Bible Commentary* Vol. 32, ed. William Foxwell Albright and David Noel Freedman, (Garden City, New York: Doubleday & Company, Inc., 1976), 166.

[16] Kathleen A. Cahalan, *Projects That Matter: Successful Planning & Evaluation for Religious Organizations,* (Herdon, Virginia: The Alban Institute, 2003), 90. Cahalan's book was written to help religious organizations plan and evaluate programming for the purpose of funding. However, the final chapter of her work, "Discerning and Prudent Stewards: Theological Perspectives on Planning and Evaluation," carries important insights regarding the interplay of leadership and discernment. pp.84-95. Smith reminds us that our discernment should be bathed in a "prayer of illumination" that the Holy Spirit would guide our individual and collective hearing of what God is inviting us to consider. Smith, *Called to Be Saints,* 194. Both Cahalan and Smith are supported by Orr and Walther as they contend, "The use of the first person plural throughout the section (of 1 Corinthians 2:14-16) suggests that the *locus operandi* of the Spirit is the fellowship of the Christian community. The examination which produces spiritual comprehension is not properly conducted by one person in isolation but in the common life of the church." Orr and Walther, *Anchor Commentary,* 166.

communal prayer and counsel, among Christians who seek together to discern what God is doing and what we are to do in response."[16] Holy leadership calls together all those involved in this Kingdom ministry, so that it can know, not only its own strengths and limits, but discern the realism of what it can accomplish with integrity as a seminary.[17]

Servanthood

Holy leadership rests firmly on the model life of Jesus. Jesus "redefines leadership and rearranges the lines of authority."[18] Leadership does not need to ask "what would Jesus do," but rather do what Jesus did. There is no mystery about what Jesus did. It is fully described in the Gospels. If those leading seminaries have paid any attention to their previous academic work in exegesis and theology, they would not need to wonder about service or Jesus' actions. It would be more of a choice to live out what the gospels narrate concerning the ministry of Jesus. Earlier it was noted that our "relationship with the divine Other" is foundational. It is out of that relationship that "true service" can grow.[19]

Holy leaders need never wonder what they are called to do as individuals or what they are to model and invite the seminary community to embody regarding service. One of the most significant passages to guide leaders is this:

---

[17] Smith, *Called to Be Saints,* 105. As a seminary, the Anderson University School of Theology has practiced this call to community discernment through regular prayer times in faculty meetings and in a structured format utilizing the book by Rose Mary Doughtery, *Group Spiritual Direction: Community Discernment,* Mahwah, New Jersey: Paulist Press, 1995. The call to community discernment is essential, but can be difficult and slow. Such processes, we found, require involvement, authenticity, grace and space, and a commitment to work and be together intentionally.

[18] Foster, 111.

[19] Foster 112. Foster continues this line of identifying "true service" by stating large and small service are indistinguishable, is "content in hiddenness," is "free of calculated results," serves all people not just a selected group, is based on need not one's mood, is a life-style, freely given, and humble, that in the end builds community. pp. 112-113.

So Jesus called them and said to them, "You know that among the Gentiles those whom they recognize as their rulers lord it over them, and their great ones are tyrants over them. But it is not so among you; but whoever wishes to become great among you must be your servant, and whoever wishes to be first among you must be slave of all. For the Son of Man came not to be served but to serve, and to give his life a ransom for many" (Mark 10:42-45, NRSV).[20]

Seminaries are collectively big business. But they are not ultimately about profit and loss, return on investments, financial resources, manufacturing a product, or the delivery of educational materials. Seminaries play a role in the Kingdom of God by forming women and men through the intertwined elements of "scholarship, spirituality, and service offered to the glory of God."[21] They are ultimately places where disciples accept the call to become "ministers of reconciliation."[22]

Holy leaders, who are ultimately spiritual leaders, understand what they undertake is a holy calling. As leadership authors and churchmen Henry and Richard Blackaby remind us, "Holding a leadership position in a Christian organization does not make one a spiritual leader. Spiritual leadership is not an occupation: it is a calling . . . Only when we understand leadership in light of God's calling on our lives will we be equipped to lead effectively."[23]

---

[20] A book useful in hearing the heart of Jesus' leadership model is Donald B. Kraybill's, *The Upside-Down Kingdom,* Kitchner, Ontario: Herald Press, 1978. Kraybill reminds us that Jesus' words call us to a radical faith practiced in what is upside-down when compared to the cultural norm. The most upside-down witness is portrayed by Jesus in the Upper Room with a towel and basin, John 13:1-20.

[21] Anderson University School of Theology catalog, (Anderson, Indiana: Anderson University), 2012, p. 3.

[22] 2 Corinthians 5:18-20 invites us to follow the apostolic witness and also become ambassadors for the ministry of reconciliation.

[23] Henry Blackaby and Richard Blackaby, *Spiritual Leadership: Moving People on to God's Agenda,* (Nashville, Tennessee: Broadman and Holman Publishers, 2001), p. xi.

Bibliography

Anderson, Leith, Personal communication, 2011.

Anselm, "Why God Became a Man," in *Anselm of Canterbury*, trans. Jasper Hopkins and Herbert Richardson, 4 vols. Toronto: Edwin Mellen, 1974.

Blackaby, Henry and Richard Blackaby. *Spiritual Leadership: Moving People on to God's Agenda.* Nashville: Broadman and Holman Publishers, 2001.

Borges, Jason. "'Dignified': An Exegetical Soteriology of Divine Honour," in *Scottish Journal of Theology* 66 (February 2013), 74-87.

Bowling, John C. *Grace-Full Leadership: Understanding the Heart of a Christian Leader.* Kansas City, Mo.: Beacon Hill Press of Kansas City, 2011.

Brand, Paul and Philip Yancey. *Fearfully and Wonderfully Made.* Grand Rapids: Zondervan, 1997.

Brooks, Phillips. *The Joy of Preaching.* Grand Rapids: Kregel, 1989.

Brown, David. "Anselm on Atonement," in *The Cambridge Companion to Anselm*, ed. Brian Davies and Brian Leftow. Cambridge: Cambridge University Press, 2004.

Brueggemann, Walter. *The Word Militant: Preaching a Decentering Word.* Minneapolis: Fortress Press, 2010.

_____. *The Practice of Prophetic Imagination: Preaching an Emancipating Word.* Minneapolis: Fortress, 2012.

Cahalan, Kathleen A. *Projects That Matter: Successful Planning & Evaluation for Religious Organizations.* Herdon, Virginia: The Alban Institute, 2003.

Cahill, Mark. *One Thing You Can't Do In Heaven.* Rockwall, TX: Biblical Discipleship Publishers, 2002-2011.

Callen, Barry L. *Enriching Mind and Spirit: A History of Higher Education in the Church of God (Anderson).* Anderson: Anderson University Press, 2007.

_____. *Faith, Learning & Life: Views from the President's Office of Anderson University.* Anderson: Anderson University and Warner Press, 1991.

_____. *Guide of Soul and Mind: The Story of Anderson University.* Anderson: Warner Press, 1992.

Childs, Brevard. *Biblical Theology in Crisis.* Philadelphia: Westminster Press, 1970.

Cho, David Yonggi. *The Fourth Dimension, Volume II.* Gainesville: Bridge-Logos, 2002.

Cooper, Burton Z. and John S. McClure. *Claiming Theology in the Pulpit.* Louisville: Westminster John Knox, 2003.

Doughtery, Rose Mary. *Group Spiritual Direction: Community Discernment.* Mahwah, New Jersey: Paulist Press, 1995.

Earley, Kevin W. *Every-Member Ministry: Spiritual Gifts and God's Design For Service.* Anderson: Warner Press, 2013.

Finalyson, R.A. "Holiness, Holy," in *New Bible Dictionary,* ed. JD Douglas. Wheaton: Tyndale, 1984.

Foster, Richard J. *Celebration of Discipline: The Path of Spiritual Growth*. New York: Harper & Row, Publishers, 1978.

Gary, Heather Grennan. "A Graceful Exit," *In Trust,* New Year 2012, accessed March 21, 2014, http://www.intrust.org/portals/39/docs/SpotlightArticle.pdf.

Hammet, Edward H. and James R. Pierce. *Reaching People Under 40 While Keeping People Over 60*. St. Louis, MO: Chalice Press, 2007.

Henson, Greg and Gary Hoag. "More Schools, Fewer Students: What's Your Seminary's Position in the Changing Market of Theological Education?" *In Trust: Center for Theological Schools* 25, no. 1, (Autumn 2013).

Hersey, Paul and Kenneth Blanchard. *Management of Organizational Behavior: Utilizing Human Resources*. Englewood Cliffs, NJ: Prentice Hall, 1996.

Howell, Brian and Jenell Williams Paris. *Introducing Cultural Anthropology: A Christian Perspective*. Grand Rapids: Baker Academic, 2011.

Kalas, Ellsworth J. *Preaching from the Soul*. Nashville: Abingdon, 2003.

Kenneth C Kinghorn, *A Celebration of Ministry: Essays in Honor of Frank Bateman Stanger*. Wilmore: Francis Asbury Publishing Company, 1982.

Kinlaw, Dennis F. *Preaching in the Spirit: A Preacher Looks for Something That Human Energy Cannot Provide*. Wilmore: Francis Asbury Society, 1985.

Kraybill, Donald B. *The Upside-Down Kingdom*. Kitchner, Ontario: Herald Press, 1978.

Lewis, Stephen R., Managing Editor. *2014 Yearbook: United States and Canada.* Anderson: Warner Press, 2014.

Management Sciences for Health, "Planning for Leadership Transition," *The Manager* (Boston), vol. 10, no. 1 (2001): 1-22.

Martin, Judith N. and Thomas K. Nakayama. *Experiencing Intercultural Communication: An Introduction.* Mountain View: Mayfield Publishing Co. 2001.

Massey, James Earl. *The Burdensome Joy of Preaching.* Nashville: Abingdon Press, 1998.

Miller, Donald. *Blue Like Jazz: Non-Religious Thoughts on Faith.* Nashville: Thomas Nelson, 2003.

Moss, Marvin Anthony. *Next: Surviving A Leadership Transition.* Nashville: Abingdon Press, 2013, Kindle Electronic Edition.

Newstadt, Leah. "Let's Go Neighboring," *Guideposts,* 1954, accessed March 1, 2014, http://homeandholidays.com/lets-go-heighboring.

Nouwen, Henri J.M. *In the Name of Jesus: Reflections on Christian Leadership.* New York: Crossroad, 1989.

Nouwen, Henri. *Creative Ministry.* New York: Image Books, 1991.

_____. *Life of the Beloved: Spiritual Living in a Secular World.* New York: Crossroads, 2001.

Orr, William F. and James Arthur Walther. "1 Corinthians," *The Anchor Bible Commentary* Vol. 32, ed. William Foxwell Albright and David Noel Freedman. Garden City, New York: Doubleday & Company, Inc., 1976.

Paese, Matt and Richard S. Wellins, "Leaders in Transition: Stepping Up, Not Off," Development Dimensions International, Inc. (2007), 1-22, accessed March 22, 2014, http://www.ddiworld.com.

Pedersen, Paul. *The Five Stages of Culture Shock: Critical Incidents Around the World*. Westport: Greenwood Press, 1995.

Peterson, Eugene. *Under the Unpredictable Plant: An Exploration in Vocational Holiness*. Grand Rapids: William B. Eerdmans, 1992.

_____. *Working the Angles: The Shape of Pastoral Integrity*. Grand Rapids: William B. Eerdmans, 1992. Publishing Co., 1987. Kindle Edition.

von Rad, Gerhard. *Biblical Interpretations in Preaching*. transl. John E. Steely. Nashville: Abingdon, 1977.

Ricoeur, Paul. *Interpretation Theory: Discourse and the Surplus of Meaning*. Fort Worth: Texas Christian University Press, 1976.

Rose, Lucy Atkinson. *Sharing the Word: Preaching in the Roundtable Church*. Louisville: Westminster John Knox, 1997.

Saccone, Steve. *Protégé: Developing Your Next Generation of Church Leaders*. Downers Grove, IL: IVP Books, 2012. Kindle Edition.

Sebastian, David L. *Recovering Our Nerve: A Primer for Evangelism in Everyday Life*. Anderson: Warner Press, 2013.

Sleeth, Ronald Eugene. "Crisis in Teaching," Perkins Journal 30, no. 4 (June 1, 1977): 1-41. ATLA Religion Database with ATLASerials, EBSCOhost (accessed April 29, 2014).

Smith, Gordon T. *Called to Be Saints: An Invitation to Christian Maturity*. Downer's Grove: Intervarsity Press, 2014.

Smith, John W.V. *I Will Build My Church: Biblical Insights on Distinguishing Doctrines of the Church of God.* Anderson: Warner Press, 1985.

Stafford, Gilbert W. *Church of God at the Crossroads.* Anderson: Warner Press, 2000.

Stanley, Andy and Lane Jones. *Communicating for Change: Seven Keys to Irresistible Communication.* Colorado Springs: Multnomah Books, 2006.

Starnes, Sr., Darryl B. *Equipping the Saints for the Work of Ministry: Teaching Adults to Share Their Faith at Evans Metropolitan African Methodist Episcopal Zion Church, Bennettsville, South Carolina.* D.Min diss., Samford University Beeson Divinity School, 1998.

Strege, Merle D. *I Saw the Church: The Life of the Church of God Told Theologically.* Anderson: Warner Press, 2002.

Taylor, Barbara Brown. "Telling Truths," *Christian Century* 123, no. 15 (July 25, 2006): 31. ATLA Religion Database with ATLASerials, EBSCOhost (accessed April 29, 2014).

Teen Mission International, "Roman Road to Salvation," accessed March 10, 2014, http://www.teenmissions.org/resources/roman-road-to-salvation.

Torrance, J.B. "Confession," in *New Bible Dictionary.* ed. JD Douglas. Wheaton: Tyndale, 1984.

Wendell, P. R. *When Leaders Leave: A New Perspective on Leadership Change.* Philadelphia: MarketShift, Inc., 2013.

Wesley, John. *The Methodist Societies: History, Nature, and Design.* The Works of John Wesley. ed. Rupert E. Davies. Nashville: Abingdon, 1989.

Wheelwright, Lorin F. "The Man Who Remembered," *The Instructor,* 1969, 234-235, accessed March 20, 2014, https://archive.org/stream/instructor1047dese#page/n7/mode/2up/search/wheelwright.

Willimon, William H. "Voice Lessons: Learning to Preach." *Christian Century* 128, no. 3 (February 8, 2011): 10-12. ATLA Religion Database with ATLASerials, EBSCOhost (accessed April 28, 2014).

_____. *Worship as Pastoral Care.* Nashville: Abingdon, 1979.

_____, and Bryan Langlands. *A Will to Lead and the Grace to Follow: Letters on Leadership from a Peculiar Prophet.* Nashville: Abingdon Press, 2011.

Wimberly, Anne Streaty, ed. *Honoring African American Elders: a Ministry in the Soul Community.* San Francisco: Jossey-Bass Publishers, 1997.

Wright, N.T. *After You Believe: Why Christian Character Matters.* New York, NY: Harper-Collins, 2010. Kindle Edition.